SRA
Reading Mastery
Signature Edition

Spelling Presentation Book
Grade 5

Robert Dixon
Siegfried Engelmann

SRA

Columbus, OH

SRAonline.com

 SRA

Send all inquiries to this address:
SRA/McGraw-Hill
4400 Easton Commons
Columbus, OH 43219

ISBN: 978-0-07-612655-2
MHID: 0-07-612655-2

2 3 4 5 6 7 8 9 10 BCM 13 12 11 10 09 08 07

Guide to *Spelling Presentation Book* Grade 5

Introduction

Present the spelling component of *Reading Mastery Signature Edition,* Grade 5, at a time other than the period for reading. In other words, spelling lessons should not infringe upon the time scheduled for reading. Each spelling lesson takes about ten to fifteen minutes, so you can use these lessons flexibly during the time allotted for language arts instruction. Spelling instruction begins with lesson 1 of the reading program and goes with each reading lesson through 120. (You present spelling lesson 1 on the same day as reading lesson 1.) Remember, reading lessons match with spelling lessons, so under no circumstances should you end up on a spelling lesson beyond the reading lesson you are teaching.

Although these spelling lessons, when taught to mastery, will markedly improve students' spelling ability, their greatest value might be that of reinforcing reading. The ability to encode a word strengthens students' ability to decode a word.

Material

You present lessons from the Grade 5 *Spelling Presentation Book.* Your students write answers for some activities on their own paper. They will need a red pen on test day (every tenth lesson).

What Is Taught?

Three Approaches to Teaching Spelling Content
Reading Mastery Signature Edition, Grade 5 *Spelling* uses three approaches to teaching spelling content: whole-word, phonemic, and morphemic. Each approach has advantages and possible disadvantages. *Reading Mastery,* Grade 5 *Spelling* combines all three approaches and is designed to maximize the advantages of each approach and minimize the disadvantages.

Whole Word

This approach requires students to memorize the spelling of individual words. Students are not taught rules but simply memorize information, such as "The word **thought** is spelled **t-h-o-u-g-h-t.**"

The advantage of the whole-word approach is that it is the only way to teach words that do not fit generalizations, such as the word **answer.**

The disadvantage of whole-word instruction is that it is inefficient. To teach two thousand words, each word must be presented as a separate entity, a rote unit that is essentially unrelated to other words being taught.

Phonemic

This approach, based on sound-symbol relationships, involves teaching students the letters for various sounds, such as "The sound **/n/** is spelled with the letter **n.**" The advantage of this approach is that it provides spellers with generalizations for spelling many words and word parts. This approach is most advantageous when applied to regular spelling words—those composed entirely of predictable, or stable, elements. For example, "The sound **/m/** is spelled with the letter **m, /a/** with **a,** and **/n/** with **n. Man**, therefore, is spelled **m-a-n.**"

One problem with this approach, as it is traditionally used, is that it confuses reading objectives with spelling objectives. Many spellings produce the sound /ē/ (e-a, e-i, e-e, e, i-e). Reading instruction teaches learners what sound to say when presented with any of these symbols; however, the problem of spelling is different.

Students are presented with a sound in a word and must produce the appropriate spelling. Which spelling is correct? A tricky balance exists. The stable elements in a word like **teen** can be spelled by applying sound-symbol generalizations. At the same time, students must be taught to avoid the overgeneralization of spelling all long-e words with **e-e.**

The phonemic approach is weakest when applied to multisyllabic words, particularly those containing an unstressed vowel that sounds like "uh" and could be spelled with any vowel letter. The "uh" in the word relative (rel-uh-tiv) could be spelled with a, e, o, or u.

Morphemic

The morphemic approach to spelling teaches students to spell units—bases and affixes—of words and to put them together to form words. The term **morphograph** applies to all these units. A morphograph is the smallest word part that has meaning. For example, **water** is made of two syllables but only one morphograph.

The primary advantage of using morphographs is that a small number of them can be combined to form a large number of words. After students have learned some morphographs, spelling words composed of more than one morphograph is relatively easy.

Most morphographs are spelled the same way in every word in which they occur. Others, such as **hope,** change their spelling in some cases. But the change, such as dropping the final **e,** is predictable and can be taught through reliable spelling rules.

The morphemic approach is most efficient for multisyllabic words. These words typically defy phonemic analysis; however, they can be effectively taught as combinations of morphographs. Five or six hundred morphographs combine to form thousands of words.

One difficulty within a morphemic approach is that learning to spell morphographs may depend on sound-symbol and whole-word analyses.

The principal focus of *Reading Mastery Signature Edition,* Grade 5 *Spelling* is upon the *morphemic* approach to spelling. At this level, students have already used phonemic spelling patterns. The morphemic emphasis of this level involves students learning numerous common prefixes and suffixes, word bases, and non-word bases, such as **cept** in the word **receptive.** The program refers to such parts collectively as *morphographs.* Students add combinations of morphographs to one another in order to create new words, and they analyze the morphographs in whole, multi-morphograph words. Sometimes combining morphographs requires students to change the spelling of one or more parts. Rules govern such changes, which the program teaches to your students.

Reading Mastery Signature Edition, Grade 5 *Spelling* also teaches students numerous irregularly spelled words, which are usually introduced in the context of sentences.

Scope and Sequence

Whole Word

Sentences Many irregularly spelled words are introduced in sentences. Students master the spelling of irregular words within the model sentence, and then variations of the sentence are presented so that students apply the spelling of those words to various sentence contexts.

Whole Words

Sentence	Lesson Introduced
People weren't interested in the photograph.	16
Anybody would rather be healthy instead of wealthy.	27
The union of physical science and logic was a major development.	36
The committee had high regard for honesty and courage.	51
Two scientists and their assistants were in an automobile accident.	66
Some explorers discovered treasure on a magic island.	71
That student appears to be thorough and conscientious.	82
Their approach to acquiring knowledge fascinates me.	94
Adequately protecting the environment is a challenge.	102

Morphemic

Prefixes and Suffixes Following is a list of lessons in which prefixes and suffixes are introduced.

Affixes	
Prefix or Suffixes	**Lesson Introduced**
-s	1, 24
-ing	1
-ed	1
-er	1, 15
-less	2
-able	3
re-	4
-ful	5
-ness	6
un-	9
-est	13
-al	14
-ly	16
de-	21
-en	22
-age	23
in-	23
con-	24
-y	25
ex-	25
-ment	26
pro-	26
-ive	28
-ion	28
-ure	29
pre-	31
-ous	33
dis-	41
-ist	42
-ic	46
-ish	51
trans-	55
ap-	58
for-	72
sub-	75
ob-	77
-ual	81
per-	83
a-	86
(ic) al (ly)	86
com-	88
-hood	92
-ate	98
be-	101
im-	106
e-	107
ad-	108
sup-	109
sur-	111
-ship	113
-ial	118

Morphemic Principles and Rules Following is a list of lessons in which morphemic principles and rules are introduced. Skills for these principles and rules are taught well in advance of the introduction of the principles and rules themselves.

Morphemic Principles and Rules

Drop the final **e** from a word when the suffix begins with a vowel letter.	6
Double the final consonant in a word that ends **CVC** when the next morphograph begins with a vowel letter.	11
Change the **y** to **i** when word ends consonant-and-y, and the next morphograph begins with anything, except **i**.	18
Add **es** instead of **s** if a word ends in **s, z, sh, ch,** or in **consonant-and-y**.	32, 35
Drop the **e** when a word ends with the letter **w** and you add **en**.	63
Add **al** when a word ends in **ic** before adding **ly**.	84
Use the doubling rule when a (multisyllabic) word ends in a short **CVC** morphograph.	103

Nonword Bases Following is a list of lessons in which nonword bases are introduced.

Nonword Bases

Base	Lesson Introduced	Example
tect	32, 34	de**tect**ive
gress	32, 35	pro**gress**
cept	32, 37	con**cept**ion
ject	33	re**ject**ion
tain	38	re**tain**er
spect	39	in**spect**ion
pel	43	re**pel**

vise	44	**vis**ion (**e** drops when adding **-ion**)
duce	47	**re**duce
duct	53	pro**duct**ion
muse	55	**mus**ic (**e** drops when adding **ic**)
fer	56	re**fer**red (**r** doubles when adding **-ed**)
tent	62	at**tent**ive
tend	71	pre**tend**
struct	76	de**struct**ive
tract	78	at**tract**ive
sist	82	in**sist**ed
fect	87	de**fect**ive
cur	89	oc**cur**red (**r** doubles when adding **-ed**)
miss	93	**miss**ion
mit	94	ad**mit** (**t** doubles)
fuse	99	re**fus**al (**e** drops when adding **-al**)
ply	102	ap**pli**ed (**y** changes to **i** when adding **-ed**)
vert	106	con**vert**ing
lief	107	be**lief**
lieve	107	re**lieve**
ceive	108	re**ceive**
sume	109	re**sume**
lent	111	re**lent**less
plete	111	com**plete**
prise	113	sur**prise**
stant	113	in**stant**ly
auto	115	**auto**mobile
tele	115	**tele**graph
sect	115	**sect**ion

mote	117	**mot**ion (**e** drops when adding **-ion**)
dict	117	pre**dict**
cise	117	in**cis**ion (**e** drops when adding **-ion**)
fess	118	con**fess**ion
stance	118	in**stance**

Assessment

You will administer a ten-word test in every tenth lesson, beginning with lesson 10. Students will need a red pen.

How the Spelling is Taught

Follow the same conventions and critical teaching practices for teaching the spelling lessons that you use for teaching the reading lessons. As in a reading lesson, utilize group responses, clear signals, and fast pacing.

Corrections

You will use a single basic correction procedure for correcting errors in the spelling lessons:
1. (Model.) Tell students the correct answer.
2. (Lead.) Say the response with students. You may need to repeat this step three to five times for all students to be firm.
3. (Test.) Check to make sure students respond correctly.
4. (Delayed test.) After students pass the test, return to the beginning of the exercise to determine if their response is firm.

Spelling Example
Students misspell a word in step c of the following sample exercise.

Spelling Review
a. Get ready to spell words.
b. Word 1 is **thought.** Spell **thought.** Get ready. (Signal.) *T-H-O-U-G-H-T.*
c. Word 2 is **friend.** Spell **friend.** Get ready. (Signal.) *F-R-E-N-D.*
[Teacher corrects here.]

Correction:
(Stop as soon as a mistake occurs.)
a. (Model.) Listen: **f-r-i-e-n-d.**
b. (Lead.) With me. Spell **friend.** Get ready. (Signal and respond with students.) *F-R-I-E-N-D.*
c. (Test.) Your turn. Spell **friend.** Get ready. (Signal.) *F-R-I-E-N-D.*
d. (Delayed test.) Spell **thought.** Get ready. (Signal.) *T-H-O-U-G-H-T.*
e. Spell **friend** again. Get ready. (Signal.) *F-R-I-E-N-D.*

Sentence Repetition Example
Students make an error repeating a sentence exactly.

Sentence Variation

a. Get ready to write on lined paper.

• You are going to write a sentence made up of words you know how to spell. Put the right punctuation mark at the end of the sentence.

b. The sentence is **Some scientists discovered an injection to increase health and strength.**

• Say that sentence. Get ready. (Signal.) *Some sciences...*

Correction:

(Stop as soon as a mistake occurs.)

a. (Model.) Listen: **Some scientists discovered an injection to increase health and strength.**

b. (Lead.) With me. Say that sentence. Get ready. (Signal and respond with students.) *Some scientists discovered an injection to increase health and strength.*

c. (Test.) Your turn. Say that sentence. Get ready. (Signal.) *Some scientists discovered an injection to increase health and strength.*

d. (Delayed test.) Again. Say that sentence. Get ready. (Signal.) *Some scientists discovered an injection to increase health and strength.*

If the error seems to be very minor—due perhaps to a lack of attention—use the same correction procedure without the "lead" step, which saves a little time. Note that the "delayed test" yields the most important diagnostic information. If your students have trouble on that step, start the basic correction procedure over and use the "lead" step three or more times. For the most difficult errors, multiple delayed tests are very effective. Use the correction procedure at other times during the lesson, during other lessons, while your students line up for recess, as students put up chairs and leave for the day, or any other time. This shows students that you think it is important for them to learn the difficult word, but moreover, gives them multiple opportunities, spread over time, to remember the correct spelling.

LESSON 1

EXERCISE 1

Word Introduction

a. (Write on the board:)

> thought
> worth
> match
> use
> power
> reason

b. Get ready to read these words.
• First word: **thought.** What word? (Signal.) *Thought.*
c. Next word: **worth.** What word? (Signal.) *Worth.*
• (Repeat for: **match, use, power, reason.**)
d. Now spell those words.
• Spell **thought.** Get ready. (Signal.) *T-H-O-U-G-H-T.*
e. Spell **worth.** Get ready. (Signal.) *W-O-R-T-H.*
• (Repeat for: **match, use, power, reason.**)
f. (Erase the board.)
• Spell the words without looking.
g. Spell **thought.** Get ready. (Signal.) *T-H-O-U-G-H-T.*
h. Spell **worth.** Get ready. (Signal.) *W-O-R-T-H.*
• (Repeat for: **match, use, power, reason.**)
i. Get ready to write those words.
j. First word: **thought.** Write it. ✔
• (Repeat for: **worth, match, use, power, reason.**)

EXERCISE 2

Affixes

a. You're going to write words on lined paper. Number your paper from 1 through 5. ✔
b. Word 1 is **power.** What word? (Signal.) *Power.*
• Write the word **power.** ✔
c. Word 2 is **reason.** What word? (Signal.) *Reason.*
• Write the word **reason.** ✔
d. Word 3 is **match.** What word? (Signal.) *Match.*
• Write the word **match.** ✔

e. Word 4 is **spell.** What word? (Signal.) *Spell.*
• Write the word **spell.** ✔
f. Word 5 is **clear.** What word? (Signal.) *Clear.*
• Write the word **clear.** ✔
g. (Write on the board:)

> 1. power + s =
> 2. reason + ing =
> 3. match + ed =
> 4. spell + er =
> 5. clear + est =

• Now you're going to add suffixes to these words.
h. After **power** write a plus sign and the letter **s.** ✔
   After **s** write an equal sign. ✔
i. Write the plus signs, suffixes, and equal signs shown for the rest of the words. ✔
j. You're going to add the suffixes to make new words.
k. Word 1 is **powers.** What word? (Signal.) *Powers.*
• Write the word **powers** after the equal sign. ✔
• (Write to show:)

> 1. power + s = powers

• Here's what you should have: **power** plus **s** equals **powers.**
l. Word 2 is **reasoning.** What word? (Signal.) *Reasoning.*
• Write the word **reasoning** after the equal sign. ✔
m. Word 3 is **matched.** What word? (Signal.) *Matched.*
• Write the word **matched** after the equal sign. ✔
n. Word 4 is **speller.** What word? (Signal.) *Speller.*
• Write the word **speller** after the equal sign. ✔
o. Word 5 is **clearest.** What word? (Signal.) *Clearest.*
• Write the word **clearest** after the equal sign. ✔
p. Check your work. Make an **X** next to any word you got wrong.

q. Word 1. Spell **powers.** Get ready. (Tap for each letter.) *P-O-W-E-R-S.*
• (Repeat for: **2. reasoning, 3. matched, 4. speller, 5. clearest.**)

Morphograph Introduction

a. (Write on the board:)

> **1. misspelled = mis + spell + ed**
>
> **2. unpacking = un + pack + ing**
>
> **3. clearer = clear + er**

b. Prefixes, suffixes, and base words can all be called **morphographs.**
c. What can you call all prefixes, suffixes, and base words? (Signal.) *Morphographs.*
• (Repeat until firm.)

d. The first **morphograph** in **misspelled** is **mis.**
• The next **morphograph** in **misspelled** is **spell.**
• The next **morphograph** in **misspelled** is **e-d.**
e. Look at word 2.
f. What's the first **morphograph** in **unpacking?** (Signal.) *Un.*
• What's the next **morphograph** in **unpacking?** (Signal.) *Pack.*
• What's the next **morphograph** in **unpacking?** (Signal.) *Ing.*
g. Look at word 3.
h. What's the first **morphograph** in **clearer?** (Signal.) *Clear.*
• What's the next **morphograph** in **clearer?** (Signal.) *Er.*
• (Give individual turns on identifying the morphographs in: **1. misspelled, 2. unpacking, 3. clearer.**)

EXERCISE 1

Affix Introduction

a. (Write on the board:)

> 1. thought + less =
> 2. match + less =
> 3. power + less =

- In these words the morphograph **less** means **without.** What does **less** mean? (Signal.) *Without.*

b. So what word means **without thought?** (Signal.) *Thoughtless.*

c. What word means **without match?** (Signal.) *Matchless.*

d. What word means **without power?** (Signal.) *Powerless.*

e. Number your paper from 1 to 3. ✔

f. Add the morphograph **less** to make new words. Write just the new words. ✔

g. Check your work. Make an **X** next to any word you got wrong.

h. Word 1. Spell **thoughtless.** Get ready. (Tap for each letter.) *T-H-O-U-G-H-T-L-E-S-S.*

- (Repeat for: **2. matchless, 3. powerless.**)

EXERCISE 2

Word Introduction

a. (Write on the board:)

> doubt
> mother
> print
> place
> price
> view

b. Get ready to read these words.

- First word: **doubt.** What word? (Signal.) *Doubt.*

c. Next word: **mother.** What word? (Signal.) *Mother.*

- (Repeat for: **print, place, price, view.**)

d. Now spell those words.

- Spell **doubt.** Get ready. (Signal.) *D-O-U-B-T.*

e. Spell **mother.** Get ready. (Signal.) *M-O-T-H-E-R.*

- (Repeat for: **print, place, price, view.**)

f. (Erase the board.)

- Spell the words without looking.

g. Spell **doubt.** Get ready. (Signal.) *D-O-U-B-T.*

h. Spell **mother.** Get ready. (Signal.) *M-O-T-H-E-R.*

- (Repeat for: **print, place, price, view.**)

i. Get ready to write those words.

j. First word: **doubt.** Write it. ✔

- (Repeat for: **mother, print, place, price, view.**)

EXERCISE 3

Prompted Review

> *Note:* Pronounce **use** so it rhymes with **juice.**

a. (Write on the board:)

> 1. power
> 2. thought
> 3. reason
> 4. worth
> 5. match
> 6. use

b. Word 1 is **power.** Spell **power.** Get ready. (Signal.) *P-O-W-E-R.*

c. Word 2 is **thought.** Spell **thought.** Get ready. (Signal.) *T-H-O-U-G-H-T.*

d. (Repeat step c for: **3. reason, 4. worth, 5. match, 6. use.**)

e. (Erase the board.)

- Now spell those words without looking.

f. Word 1 is **power.** Spell **power.** Get ready. (Signal.) *P-O-W-E-R.*

g. Word 2 is **thought.** Spell **thought.** Get ready. (Signal.) *T-H-O-U-G-H-T.*

h. (Repeat step g for: **3. reason, 4. worth, 5. match, 6. use.**)

i. (Give individual turns on: **1. power, 2. thought, 3. reason, 4. worth, 5. match, 6. use.**)

EXERCISE 1

Affix Introduction

a. (Write on the board:)

> 1. print + able =
> 2. reach + able =
> 3. stretch + able =

- In these words the morphograph **able** means **able to be.** What does **able** mean? (Signal.) *Able to be.*

b. So what word means **able to be printed?** (Signal.) *Printable.*

c. What word means **able to be reached?** (Signal.) *Reachable.*

d. What word means **able to be stretched?** (Signal.) *Stretchable.*

e. Number your paper from 1 to 3. ✔

f. Add the morphograph **able** to make new words. Write just the new words. ✔

g. Check your work. Make an **X** next to any word you got wrong.

h. Word 1. Spell **printable.** Get ready. (Tap for each letter.) *P-R-I-N-T-A-B-L-E.*

- (Repeat for: **2. reachable, 3. stretchable.**)

EXERCISE 2

Word Introduction

a. (Write on the board:) WK2

> cover
> like
> cure
> move
> fresh
> sense

b. Get ready to read these words.

- First word: **cover.** What word? (Signal.) *Cover.*

c. Next word: **like.** What word? (Signal.) *Like.*

- (Repeat for: **cure, move, fresh, sense.**)

d. Now spell those words.

- Spell **cover.** Get ready. (Signal.) *C-O-V-E-R.*

e. Spell **like.** Get ready. (Signal.) *L-I-K-E.*

- (Repeat for: **cure, move, fresh, sense.**)

f. (Erase the board.)

- Spell the words without looking.

g. Spell **cover.** Get ready. (Signal.) *C-O-V-E-R.*

h. Spell **like.** Get ready. (Signal.) *L-I-K-E.*

- (Repeat for: **cure, move, fresh, sense.**)

i. Get ready to write those words.

j. First word: **cover.** Write it. ✔

- (Repeat for: **like, cure, move, fresh, sense.**)

EXERCISE 3

Prompted Review

a. (Write on the board:)

> 1. mother
> 2. thoughtless
> 3. doubt
> 4. reasoning
> 5. worthless
> 6. view

b. Word 1 is **mother.** Spell **mother.** Get ready. (Signal.) *M-O-T-H-E-R.*

c. Word 2 is **thoughtless.** Spell **thoughtless.** Get ready. (Signal.) *T-H-O-U-G-H-T-L-E-S-S.*

d. (Repeat step c for: **3. doubt, 4. reasoning, 5. worthless, 6. view.**)

e. (Erase the board.)

- Now spell those words without looking.

f. Word 1 is **mother.** Spell **mother.** Get ready. (Signal.) *M-O-T-H-E-R.*

g. Word 2 is **thoughtless.** Spell **thoughtless.** Get ready. (Signal.) *T-H-O-U-G-H-T-L-E-S-S.*

h. (Repeat step g for: **3. doubt, 4. reasoning, 5. worthless, 6. view.**)

i. (Give individual turns on: **1. mother, 2. thoughtless, 3. doubt, 4. reasoning, 5. worthless, 6. view.**)

EXERCISE 1

Affix Introduction

a. (Write on the board:)

> 1. re + late =
> 2. re + strain =
> 3. re + turn =

- All these words have the morphograph **re.**
b. Number your paper from 1 to 3. ✔
c. Add the morphographs together to make new words. Write just the new words. ✔
d. Check your work. Make an **X** next to any word you got wrong.
e. Word 1. Spell **relate.** Get ready. (Tap for each letter.) *R-E-L-A-T-E.*
- (Repeat for: **2. restrain, 3. return.**)

EXERCISE 2

Word Introduction

a. (Write on the board:) WK 3

> sound
> quote
> guide
> name
> base
> sore

b. Get ready to read these words.
- First word: **sound.** What word? (Signal.) *Sound.*
c. Next word: **quote.** What word? (Signal.) *Quote.*
- (Repeat for: **guide, name, base, sore.**)
d. Now spell those words.
- Spell **sound.** Get ready. (Signal.) *S-O-U-N-D.*
e. Spell **quote.** Get ready. (Signal.) *Q-U-O-T-E.*
- (Repeat for: **guide, name, base, sore.**)
f. (Erase the board.)
- Spell the words without looking.

g. Spell **sound.** Get ready. (Signal.) *S-O-U-N-D.*
h. Spell **quote.** Get ready. (Signal.) *Q-U-O-T-E.*
- (Repeat for: **guide, name, base, sore.**)
i. Get ready to write those words.
j. First word: **sound.** Write it. ✔
- (Repeat for: **quote, guide, name, base, sore.**)

EXERCISE 3

Prompted Review

a. (Write on the board:) WK 2

> 1. viewable
> 2. remove
> 3. doubtless
> 4. thought
> 5. straining
> 6. stretchable

b. Word 1 is **viewable.** Spell **viewable.** Get ready. (Signal.) *V-I-E-W-A-B-L-E.*
c. Word 2 is **remove.** Spell **remove.** Get ready. (Signal.) *R-E-M-O-V-E.*
d. (Repeat step c for: **3. doubtless, 4. thought, 5. straining, 6. stretchable.**)
e. (Erase the board.)
- Now spell those words without looking.
f. Word 1 is **viewable.** Spell **viewable.** Get ready. (Signal.) *V-I-E-W-A-B-L-E.*
g. Word 2 is **remove.** Spell **remove.** Get ready. (Signal.) *R-E-M-O-V-E.*
h. (Repeat step g for: **3. doubtless, 4. thought, 5. straining, 6. stretchable.**)
i. (Give individual turns on: **1. viewable, 2. remove, 3. doubtless, 4. thought, 5. straining, 6. stretchable.**)

EXERCISE 1

Affix Introduction

a. (Write on the board:)

> 1. doubt + ful =
> 2. power + ful =
> 3. pain + ful =

- In these words the morphograph **ful** means **full of.** What does **ful** mean? (Signal.) *Full of.*
b. So what word means **full of doubt?** (Signal.) *Doubtful.*
c. What word means **full of power?** (Signal.) *Powerful.*
d. What word means **full of pain?** (Signal.) *Painful.*
e. Number your paper from 1 to 3. ✔
f. Add the morphograph **ful** to make new words. Just write the new words. ✔
g. Check your work. Make an **X** next to any word you got wrong.
h. Word 1. Spell **doubtful.** Get ready. (Tap for each letter.) *D-O-U-B-T-F-U-L.*
- (Repeat for: **2. powerful, 3. painful.**)

EXERCISE 2

Morphographic Analysis

a. (Write on the board:)

> 1. restrain =
> 2. stretchable =
> 3. reviewer =
> 4. powerless =
> 5. thoughtful =
> 6. returning =

- These words are made up of more than one morphograph. You're going to write the morphographs in each word, after the equal sign.
b. **Restrain.** What's the first morphograph in **restrain?** (Signal.) *Re.*
c. Write **re** and a plus sign after the equal sign. ✔
d. What's the next morphograph in **restrain?** (Signal.) *Strain.*
e. Write **strain.** ✔

f. Your paper should look like this:
- (Change the board to show:)

> 1. restrain = re + strain
> 2. stretchable =
> 3. reviewer =
> 4. powerless =
> 5. thoughtful =
> 6. returning =

g. Do the rest of the words on your own. ✔
- (Change the board to show:)

> 1. restrain = re + strain
> 2. stretchable = stretch + able
> 3. reviewer = re + view + er
> 4. powerless = power + less
> 5. thoughtful = thought + ful
> 6. returning = re + turn + ing

h. Check your work. Make an **X** next to any word you got wrong.

EXERCISE 3

Spelling Review

a. Get ready to spell words.
b. Word 1 is **doubtful.**
- What word? (Signal.) *Doubtful.*
- Spell **doubtful.** Get ready. (Signal.) *D-O-U-B-T-F-U-L.*
c. Word 2 is **returning.**
- What word? (Signal.) *Returning.*
- Spell **returning.** Get ready. (Signal.) *R-E-T-U-R-N-I-N-G.*
d. (Repeat step c for: **3. reasonable, 4. worthless, 5. mothering, 6. soundless.**)
e. (Give individual turns on **1. doubtful, 2. returning, 3. reasonable, 4. worthless, 5. mothering, 6. soundless.**)

EXERCISE 1

Affix Introduction

a. (Write on the board:)

> 1. kind + ness =
> 2. bright + ness =
> 3. weak + ness =

- All these words have the morphograph **ness.**
b. Number your paper from 1 to 3. ✔
c. Add the morphographs together to make new words. Write just the new words. ✔
d. Check your work. Make an **X** next to any word you got wrong.
e. Word 1. Spell **kindness.** Get ready. (Tap for each letter.) *K-I-N-D-N-E-S-S.*
- (Repeat for: **2. brightness, 3. weakness.**)

EXERCISE 2

Final e Words

a. (Write on the board:)

> base + ing =
>
> base + less =

b. When we add a suffix to a word that ends with **e,** we sometimes have to change the spelling of that word.
- Here is the rule: Drop the **e** from the word when the suffix begins with a vowel letter.
c. (Point to **ing** on the board:) Does this suffix begin with a vowel letter or a consonant letter? (Signal.) *A vowel letter.*
- (Change the board to show:)

>   v
> base + ing =
>
> base + less =

d. The suffix **ing** begins with a vowel letter, so we have to drop the **e** from **base** when we add **ing.**
- (Write to show:)

>   v
> base + ing = basing
>
> base + less =

e. (Point to **less** on the board:) Does this suffix begin with a vowel letter or a consonant letter? (Signal.) *A consonant letter.*
- (Write to show:)

>   v
> base + ing = basing
>   c
> base + less =

f. The suffix **less** does not begin with a vowel letter, so we don't have to drop the **e** from **base** when we add **less.**
- (Write to show:)

>   v
> base + ing = basing
>   c
> base + less = baseless

g. Everyone, spell **basing.** Get ready. (Signal.) *B-A-S-I-N-G.*
h. Now spell **baseless.** Get ready. (Signal.) *B-A-S-E-L-E-S-S.*

Word Building

a. (Write on the board:)

> 1. thought + less = _____
> 2. stretch + able = _____
> 3. re + turn + ing = _____
> 4. pain + ful = _____
> 5. power + less = _____
> 6. sound + ness = _____

b. You're going to write the words that go in the blanks.

• Number your paper from 1 to 6. ✔

c. Word 1. Write **thoughtless** on your paper. ✔

d. Do the rest of the words on your own. ✔

e. Check your work. Make an **X** next to any word you got wrong.

f. Word 1. Spell **thoughtless.** Get ready. (Tap for each letter.) *T-H-O-U-G-H-T-L-E-S-S.*

• (Repeat for: **2. stretchable, 3. returning, 4. painful, 5. powerless, 6. soundness.**)

LESSON 7

EXERCISE 1

Word Introduction

a. (Write on the board:)

> breath
> fashion
> fair
> solve
> source
> tribe

b. Get ready to read these words.
- First word: **breath.** What word? (Signal.) *Breath.*
c. Next word: **fashion.** What word? (Signal.) *Fashion.*
- (Repeat for: **fair, solve, source, tribe.**)
d. Now spell those words.
- Spell **breath.** Get ready. (Signal.) *B-R-E-A-T-H.*
e. Spell **fashion.** Get ready. (Signal.) *F-A-S-H-I-O-N.*
- (Repeat for: **fair, solve, source, tribe.**)
f. (Erase the board.)
- Spell the words without looking.
g. Spell **breath.** Get ready. (Signal.) *B-R-E-A-T-H.*
h. Spell **fashion.** Get ready. (Signal.) *F-A-S-H-I-O-N.*
- (Repeat for: **fair, solve, source, tribe.**)
i. Get ready to write those words.
j. First word: **breath.** Write it. ✔
- (Repeat for: **fashion, fair, solve, source, tribe.**)

EXERCISE 2

Final e Words

a. (Write on the board:)

> price + ing =
>
> price + less =

b. When we add a suffix to a word that ends with **e,** we sometimes have to change the spelling of that word.
- Here is the rule: Drop the **e** from the word when the suffix begins with a vowel letter.

c. (Point to **ing** on the board:) Does this suffix begin with a vowel letter or a consonant letter? (Signal.) *A vowel letter.*
- (Change the board to show:)

> v
> price + ing =
>
> price + less =

d. The suffix **ing** begins with a vowel letter, so we have to drop the **e** from **price** when we add **ing.**
- (Write to show:)

> v
> price + ing = pricing
>
> price + less =

e. (Point to **less** on the board:) Does this suffix begin with a vowel letter or a consonant letter? (Signal.) *A consonant letter.*
- (Write to show:)

> v
> price + ing = pricing
> c
> price + less

f. The suffix **less** does not begin with a vowel letter, so we don't have to drop the **e** from **price** when we add **less.**
- (Write to show:)

> v
> price + ing = pricing
> c
> price + less = priceless

g. Everyone, spell **pricing.** Get ready. (Signal.) *P-R-I-C-I-N-G.*
h. Now spell **priceless.** Get ready. (Signal.) *P-R-I-C-E-L-E-S-S.*

EXERCISE 3

Prompted Review

a. (Write on the board:)

> 1. stretching
> 2. thoughtful
> 3. powerless
> 4. returned
> 5. doubtless
> 6. recover

b. Word 1 is **stretching.** Spell **stretching.**
Get ready. (Signal.) *S-T-R-E-T-C-H-I-N-G.*

c. Word 2 is **thoughtful.** Spell **thoughtful.**
Get ready. (Signal.) *T-H-O-U-G-H-T-F-U-L.*

d. (Repeat step c for: **3. powerless,
4. returned, 5. doubtless, 6. recover.**)

e. (Erase the board.)

• Now spell those words without looking.

f. Word 1 is **stretching.** Spell **stretching.**
Get ready. (Signal.) *S-T-R-E-T-C-H-I-N-G.*

g. Word 2 is **thoughtful.** Spell **thoughtful.**
Get ready. (Signal.) *T-H-O-U-G-H-T-F-U-L.*

h. (Repeat step g for: **3. powerless,
4. returned, 5. doubtless, 6. recover.**)

i. (Give individual turns on: **1. stretching,
2. thoughtful, 3. powerless, 4. returned,
5. doubtless, 6. recover.**)

LESSON 8

Word Building

a. (Write on the board:)

> 1. thought + less + ness = _____
> 2. fashion + able = _____
> 3. kind + ness = _____
> 4. match + less = _____
> 5. power + ful = _____
> 6. re + fresh = _____

b. You're going to write the words that go in the blanks.
- Number your paper from 1 to 6. ✔
c. Word 1. Write **thoughtlessness** on your paper. ✔
d. Do the rest of the words on your own. ✔
e. Check your work. Make an **X** next to any word you got wrong.
f. Word 1. Spell **thoughtlessness**. Get ready. (Tap for each letter.) *T-H-O-U-G-H-T-L-E-S-S-N-E-S-S.*
- (Repeat for: **2. fashionable, 3. kindness, 4. matchless, 5. powerful, 6. refresh.**)

Final e Rule

a. (Write on the board:)

> 1. use + able =
>
> 2. use + less =
>
> 3. guide + ed =
>
> 4. sore + ness =
>
> 5. name + less =
>
> 6. fair + est =

b. Number your paper from 1 through 6. ✔ Write these words and suffixes on your paper with the plus and equal signs. ✔
c. When do you drop the **e** from a word? (Signal.) *When the suffix begins with a vowel letter.*
d. Do these words on your own. Some of these words follow the final **e** rule. ✔

e. Check your work. Make an **X** next to any word you got wrong.
f. Word 1. Spell **usable.** Get ready. (Tap for each letter.) *U-S-A-B-L-E.*
- (Repeat for: **2. useless, 3. guided, 4. soreness, 5. nameless, 6. fairest.**)

Spelling Review

a. Get ready to spell words.
b. Word 1 is **weakness.**
- What word? (Signal.) *Weakness.*
- Spell **weakness.** Get ready. (Signal.) *W-E-A-K-N-E-S-S.*
c. Word 2 is **worthlessness.**
- What word? (Signal.) *Worthlessness.*
- Spell **worthlessness.** Get ready. (Signal.) *W-O-R-T-H-L-E-S-S-N-E-S-S.*
d. (Repeat step c for: **3. mother, 4. review, 5. powerful, 6. resource.**)
e. (Give individual turns on: **1. weakness, 2. worthlessness, 3. mother, 4. review, 5. powerful, 6. resource.**)

EXERCISE 1

Word Introduction

a. (Write on the board:)

> rich
> sign
> globe
> valve
> store
> scribe

b. Get ready to read these words.
- First word: **rich.** What word? (Signal.) *Rich.*
c. Next word: **sign.** What word? (Signal.) *Sign.*
- (Repeat for: **globe, valve, store, scribe.**)
d. Now spell those words.
- Spell **rich.** Get ready. (Signal.) *R-I-C-H.*
e. Spell **sign.** Get ready. (Signal.) *S-I-G-N.*
- (Repeat for: **globe, valve, store, scribe.**)
f. (Erase the board.)
- Spell the words without looking.
g. Spell **rich.** Get ready. (Signal.) *R-I-C-H.*
h. Spell **sign.** Get ready. (Signal.) *S-I-G-N.*
- (Repeat for: **globe, valve, store, scribe.**)
i. Get ready to write those words.
j. First word: **rich.** Write it. ✔
- (Repeat for: **sign, globe, valve, store, scribe.**)

EXERCISE 2

Affix Introduction

a. (Write on the board:)

> 1. un + happy =
> 2. un + fair =
> 3. un + cover =

- All these words have the morphograph **un.**
b. Number your paper from 1 to 3. ✔
c. Add the morphographs together to make new words. Write just the new words. ✔
d. Check your work. Make an **X** next to any word you got wrong.
e. Word 1. Spell **unhappy.** Get ready. (Tap for each letter.) *U-N-H-A-P-P-Y.*
- (Repeat for: **2. unfair, 3. uncover.**)

EXERCISE 3

Prompted Review

a. (Write on the board:)

> 1. solving
> 2. usable
> 3. reviewing
> 4. curable
> 5. uncured
> 6. thoughtless

b. Word 1 is **solving.** Spell **solving.** Get ready. (Signal.) *S-O-L-V-I-N-G.*
c. Word 2 is **usable.** Spell **usable.** Get ready. (Signal.) *U-S-A-B-L-E.*
d. (Repeat step c for: **3. reviewing, 4. curable, 5. uncured, 6. thoughtless.**)
e. (Erase the board.)
- Now spell those words without looking.
f. Word 1 is **solving.** Spell **solving.** Get ready. (Signal.) *S-O-L-V-I-N-G.*
g. Word 2 is **usable.** Spell **usable.** Get ready. (Signal.) *U-S-A-B-L-E.*
h. (Repeat step g for: **3. reviewing, 4. curable, 5. uncured, 6. thoughtless.**)
i. (Give individual turns on: **1. solving, 2. usable, 3. reviewing, 4. curable, 5. uncured, 6. thoughtless.**)

LESSON 10

EXERCISE 1

> *Note:* In step e, students will need a red pen
> (or colored pencil).

Test

a. Today you have a spelling test. Number your lined paper from 1 through 10. ✔

b. Word 1 is **stretchable.** What word? (Signal.) *Stretchable.*

  • Write the word **stretchable.** ✔

c. Word 2 is **painful.** What word? (Signal.) *Painful.*

  • Write the word **painful.** ✔

d. (Repeat step c for: **3. returned, 4. thoughtless, 5. mothering, 6. guide, 7. pricing, 8. recover, 9. power, 10. matchless.**)

e. Pick up your red pen. ✔
    Make an **X** next to any word you spelled wrong.

  • (Write on the board:)

1. stretchable	6. guide
2. painful	7. pricing
3. returned	8. recover
4. thoughtless	9. power
5. mothering	10. matchless

  • Write the correct spelling next to any word you spelled wrong.
     (Observe students and give feedback.)

LESSON 11

EXERCISE 1

Word Introduction

a. (Write on the board:)

> length
> strength
> fright
> tough
> shoot
> loose

b. Get ready to read these words.
- First word: **length.** What word? (Signal.) *Length.*
c. Next word: **strength.** What word? (Signal.) *Strength.*
- (Repeat for: **fright, tough, shoot, loose.**)
d. Now spell those words.
- Spell **length.** Get ready. (Signal.) *L-E-N-G-T-H.*
e. Spell **strength.** Get ready. (Signal.) *S-T-R-E-N-G-T-H.*
- (Repeat for: **fright, tough, shoot, loose.**)
f. (Erase the board.)
- Spell the words without looking.
g. Spell **length.** Get ready. (Signal.) *L-E-N-G-T-H.*
h. Spell **strength.** Get ready. (Signal.) *S-T-R-E-N-G-T-H.*
- (Repeat for: **fright, tough, shoot, loose.**)
i. Get ready to write those words.
j. First word: **length.** Write it. ✔
- (Repeat for: **strength, fright, tough, shoot, loose.**)

EXERCISE 2

Doubling Rule

a. (Write on the board:)

> spot + ing =
>
> spot + less =

b. When we add a morphograph to a word that ends with **consonant-vowel-consonant,** we sometimes have to change the spelling of that word.

c. Here is the rule: Double the final consonant when the next morphograph begins with a vowel letter.
d. My turn: When do you double the final consonant? When the next morphograph begins with a vowel letter.
e. Your turn: When do you double the final consonant? (Signal.) *When the next morphograph begins with a vowel letter.*
f. That's right, when the next morphograph begins with a vowel letter.
g. (Point to **ing** on the board:)
- Does **ing** begin with a vowel letter or a consonant letter? (Signal.) *A vowel letter.*
h. (Write to show:)

> v
> **spot + ing =**
>
> **spot + less =**

i. The morphograph **ing** begins with a vowel letter, so we have to double the final consonant in **spot** when we add **ing.**
j. (Write to show:)

> v   ↓
> **spot + ing = spotting**
>
> **spot + less =**

k. (Point to **less** on the board:)
- Does **less** begin with a vowel letter or a consonant letter? (Signal.) *A consonant letter.*
l. (Write to show:)

> v   ↓
> **spot + ing = spotting**
> c
> **spot + less =**

m. The morphograph **less** does not begin with a vowel letter, so we don't have to double the final consonant in **spot** when we add **less.**

n. (Write to show:)

$$v \qquad \downarrow$$
$$\text{spot} + \text{ing} = \text{spotting}$$
$$c$$
$$\text{spot} + \text{less} = \text{spotless}$$

o. Everyone, spell **spotting.** Get ready. (Tap for each letter.) *S-P-O-T-T-I-N-G.*

p. Now spell **spotless.** Get ready. (Tap for each letter.) *S-P-O-T-L-E-S-S.*

EXERCISE 3
Prompted Review

a. (Write on the board:)

> 1. signs
> 2. fashionable
> 3. unhappy
> 4. thoughtlessness
> 5. usable
> 6. baseless

b. Word 1 is **signs.** Spell **signs.** Get ready. (Signal.) *S-I-G-N-S.*

c. Word 2 is **fashionable.** Spell **fashionable.** Get ready. (Signal.) *F-A-S-H-I-O-N-A-B-L-E.*

d. (Repeat step c for: **3. unhappy, 4. thoughtlessness, 5. usable, 6. baseless.**)

e. (Erase the board.)

• Now spell those words without looking.

f. Word 1 is **signs.** Spell **signs.** Get ready. (Signal.) *S-I-G-N-S.*

g. Word 2 is **fashionable.** Spell **fashionable.** Get ready. (Signal.) *F-A-S-H-I-O-N-A-B-L-E.*

h. (Repeat step g for: **3. unhappy, 4. thoughtlessness, 5. usable, 6. baseless.**)

i. (Give individual turns on: **1. signs, 2. fashionable, 3. unhappy, 4. thoughtlessness, 5. usable, 6. baseless.**)

EXERCISE 1

Y as a Vowel Letter

a. (Write on the board:)

> y

b. **Y** is usually a consonant letter, but sometimes it's a vowel letter.
c. Here is the rule: If **y** is at the end of a morphograph, then it is a vowel letter.
• Listen again: (Repeat the rule.)
d. (Change the board to show:)

> y
> 1. happy
> 2. boy
> 3. you
> 4. yellow
> 5. berry
> 6. play

e. Number 1 is **happy.**
• Is the **y** a vowel letter or a consonant letter in the word **happy?** (Signal.) *A vowel letter.*
• How do you know? (Signal.) *It's at the end of a morphograph.*
f. Number 2 is **boy.**
• Is the **y** a vowel letter or a consonant letter in the word **boy?** (Signal.) *A vowel letter.*
• How do you know? (Signal.) *It's at the end of a morphograph.*
g. Number 3 is **you.**
• Is the **y** a vowel letter or a consonant letter in the word **you?** (Signal.) *A consonant letter.*
• How do you know? (Signal.) *It's not at the end of a morphograph.*
h. (Repeat step g for: **4. yellow, 5. berry, 6. play.**)

EXERCISE 2

Doubling Rule

a. (Write on the board:)

> 1. fret + ing =
>
> 2. mad + ness =
>
> 3. sun + y =
>
> 4. grab + ed =
>
> 5. fad + ish =
>
> 6. snug + ness =

b. Number your paper from 1 through 6. ✔ Copy the board on your paper with the plus and equal signs. ✔
c. Remember, when we add a morphograph to a word that ends **CVC,** we sometimes have to change the spelling of that word.
• Here is the rule: Double the final consonant when the next morphograph begins with a vowel letter.
d. When do you double the final consonant? (Signal.) *When the next morphograph begins with a vowel letter.*
e. That's right, when the next morphograph begins with a vowel letter.
f. (Point to **ing** on the board:)
• Does this suffix begin with a vowel letter or a consonant letter? (Signal.) *A vowel letter.*
g. The morphograph **ing** begins with a vowel letter, so we have to double the final consonant in **fret** when we add **ing.**
h. Write **fretting** after the equal sign for word 1. ✔
i. Finish the words on your own. ✔
j. Check your work. Make an **X** next to any word you got wrong.
k. Word 1. Spell **fretting.** Get ready. (Tap for each letter.) *F-R-E-T-T-I-N-G.*
• (Repeat for: **2. madness, 3. sunny, 4. grabbed, 5. faddish, 6. snugness.**)

Word Building

a. (Write on the board:)

> **1. un + fair + ness = _____**
> **2. re + name + ing = _____**
> **3. stretch + able = _____**
> **4. power + ful = _____**
> **5. breath + less = _____**
> **6. re + fresh + ing = _____**

b. You're going to write the words that go in the blanks.

• Some of these words follow the final **e** rule. Be careful.

• Number your paper from 1 to 6. ✔

c. Word 1. Write **unfairness** on your paper. ✔

d. Do the rest of the words on your own. ✔

e. Check your work. Make an **X** next to any word you got wrong.

f. Word 1. Spell **unfairness.** Get ready. (Tap for each letter.) *U-N-F-A-I-R-N-E-S-S.*

• (Repeat for: **2. renaming, 3. stretchable, 4. powerful, 5. breathless, 6. refreshing.**)

EXERCISE 1

Affix Introduction

a. (Write on the board:)

> 1. tough + est =
> 2. rich + est =
> 3. fair + est =

- All these words have the morphograph **est.**
b. Number your paper from 1 to 3. ✔
c. Add the morphographs together to make new words. Write just the new words. ✔
d. Check your work. Make an **X** next to any word you got wrong.
e. Word 1. Spell **toughest.** Get ready. (Tap for each letter.) *T-O-U-G-H-E-S-T.*
- (Repeat for: **2. richest, 3. fairest.**)

EXERCISE 2

Doubling Rule

a. (Write on the board:)

> 1. skid + ed =
>
> 2. star + less =
>
> 3. spot + ing =
>
> 4. flat + ness =
>
> 5. step + ed =
>
> 6. job + less =

b. Number your paper from 1 through 6. ✔ Copy the board on your paper with the plus and equal signs. ✔
c. Remember, when we add a morphograph to a word that ends **CVC,** we sometimes have to change the spelling of that word.
- Here is the rule: Double the final consonant when the next morphograph begins with a vowel letter.
d. When do you double the final consonant? (Signal.) *When the next morphograph begins with a vowel letter.*
e. That's right, when the next morphograph begins with a vowel letter.

f. (Point to **ed** on the board:)
- Does this suffix begin with a vowel letter or a consonant letter? (Signal.) *A vowel letter.*
g. The morphograph **ed** begins with a vowel letter, so we have to double the final consonant in **skid** when we add **ed.**
h. Write **skidded** after the equal sign for word 1. ✔
i. Finish the words on your own. ✔
j. Check your work. Make an **X** next to any word you got wrong.
k. Word 1. Spell **skidded.** Get ready. (Tap for each letter.) *S-K-I-D-D-E-D.*
- (Repeat for: **2. starless, 3. spotting, 4. flatness, 5. stepped, 6. jobless.**)

EXERCISE 3

Spelling Review

a. Get ready to spell words.
b. Word 1 is **soreness.**
- What word? (Signal.) *Soreness.*
- Spell **soreness.** Get ready. (Signal.) *S-O-R-E-N-E-S-S.*
c. Word 2 is **richer.**
- What word? (Signal.) *Richer.*
- Spell **richer.** Get ready. (Signal.) *R-I-C-H-E-R.*
d. (Repeat step c for: **3. value, 4. hoping, 5. reviewer, 6. sign.**)
e. (Give individual turns on: **1. soreness, 2. richer, 3. value, 4. hoping, 5. reviewer, 6. sign.**)

LESSON 14

EXERCISE 1

Affix Introduction

a. (Write on the board:)

> 1. form + al =
> 2. sign + al =
> 3. rent + al =

- All these words have the morphograph **a-l.**
b. Number your paper from 1 to 3. ✔
c. Add the morphographs together to make new words. Write just the new words. ✔
d. Check your work. Make an **X** next to any word you got wrong.
e. Word 1. Spell **formal.** Get ready. (Tap for each letter.) *F-O-R-M-A-L.*
- (Repeat for: **2. signal, 3. rental.**)

EXERCISE 2

Consonant-and-Y

a. In a few days, you are going to learn about words that end with **consonant-and-y.**
b. (Write on the board:)

> 1. study
> 2. play
> 3. pity
> 4. hurry

c. (Point to the **d** in **study.**)
- Everyone, is this a vowel letter or a consonant letter? (Signal.) *A consonant letter.*
d. **D** is a consonant letter, so **study** ends **consonant-and-y.**
e. (Point to the **a** in **play.**)
- Everyone, is this a vowel letter or a consonant letter? (Signal.) *A vowel letter.*
f. **A** is a vowel letter, so **play** does not end **consonant-and-y.**
g. (Point to the **t** in **pity.**)
- Everyone, is this a vowel letter or a consonant letter? (Signal.) *A consonant letter.*
h. **T** is a consonant letter, so **pity** ends **consonant-and-y.**
i. (Point to the **r** in **hurry.**)
- Everyone, is this a vowel letter or a consonant letter? (Signal.) *A consonant letter.*
j. **R** is a consonant letter, so **hurry** ends **consonant-and-y.**

EXERCISE 3

Prompted Review

a. (Write on the board:)

> 1. valuable
> 2. rethought
> 3. freshest
> 4. storing
> 5. scribe
> 6. flattest

b. Word 1 is **valuable.** Spell **valuable.** Get ready. (Signal.) *V-A-L-U-A-B-L-E.*
c. Word 2 is **rethought.** Spell **rethought.** Get ready. (Signal.) *R-E-T-H-O-U-G-H-T.*
d. (Repeat step c for: **3. freshest, 4. storing, 5. scribe, 6. flattest.**)
e. (Erase the board.)
- Now write those words without looking.
f. Word 1 is **valuable.** Write **valuable.** ✔
g. Word 2 is **rethought.** Write **rethought.** ✔
h. (Repeat step g for: **3. freshest, 4. storing, 5. scribe, 6. flattest.**)
i. (Check and correct.)

LESSON 15

EXERCISE 1

Affix Introduction

a. (Write on the board:)

> 1. farm + er =
> 2. fresh + er =
> 3. light + er =
> 4. help + er =

- All these words have the morphograph **e-r.**
b. Number your paper from 1 to 4. ✔
c. Add the morphographs together to make new words. Write just the new words. ✔
d. Check your work. Make an **X** next to any word you got wrong.
e. Word 1. Spell **farmer.** Get ready. (Tap for each letter.) *F-A-R-M-E-R.*
- (Repeat for: **2. fresher, 3. lighter, 4. helper.**)

EXERCISE 2

Consonant-and-Y

a. In a few days, you are going to learn about words that end with **consonant-and-y.**
b. (Write on the board:)

> 1. rusty
> 2. deny
> 3. money
> 4. stormy

c. (Point to the **t** in **rusty.**)
- Everyone, is this a vowel letter or a consonant letter? (Signal.) *A consonant letter.*
d. **T** is a consonant letter, so **rusty** ends **consonant-and-y.**
e. (Point to the **n** in **deny.**)
- Everyone, is this a vowel letter or a consonant letter? (Signal.) *A consonant letter.*
f. **N** is a consonant letter, so **deny** ends **consonant-and-y.**
g. (Point to the **e** in **money.**)
- Everyone, is this a vowel letter or a consonant letter? (Signal.) *A vowel letter.*
h. **E** is a vowel letter, so **money** does not end **consonant-and-y.**
i. (Point to the **m** in **stormy.**)

- Everyone, is this a vowel letter or a consonant letter? (Signal.) *A consonant letter.*
j. **M** is a consonant letter, so **stormy** ends **consonant-and-y.**

EXERCISE 3

Prompted Review

a. (Write on the board:)

> 1. signal
> 2. richer
> 3. shopper
> 4. nameless
> 5. strength
> 6. fashionable

b. Word 1 is **signal.** Spell **signal.** Get ready. (Signal.) *S-I-G-N-A-L.*
c. Word 2 is **richer.** Spell **richer.** Get ready. (Signal.) *R-I-C-H-E-R.*
d. (Repeat step c for: **3. shopper, 4. nameless, 5. strength, 6. fashionable.**)
e. (Erase the board.)
- Now spell those words without looking.
f. Word 1 is **signal.** Spell **signal.** Get ready. (Signal.) *S-I-G-N-A-L.*
g. Word 2 is **richer.** Spell **richer.** Get ready. (Signal.) *R-I-C-H-E-R.*
h. (Repeat step g for: **3. shopper, 4. nameless, 5. strength, 6. fashionable.**)
i. (Give individual turns on: **1. signal, 2. richer, 3. shopper, 4. nameless, 5. strength, 6. fashionable.**)

LESSON 16

EXERCISE 1

Sentence

a. (Write on the board:)

> **People weren't interested in the photograph.**

- I'll read the sentence on the board: **People weren't interested in the photograph.**
- Let's spell some of those words.

b. Spell **People.** Get ready. (Signal.) *P-E-O-P-L-E.*
- Spell **weren't.** Get ready. (Signal.) *W-E-R-E-N-apostrophe-T.*
- Spell **interested.** Get ready. (Signal.) *I-N-T-E-R-E-S-T-E-D.*
- Spell **photograph.** Get ready. (Signal.) *P-H-O-T-O-G-R-A-P-H.*

c. Copy this sentence on lined paper.

d. (Pause, then check and correct.)
- Read the sentence you just copied. Get ready. (Signal.) *People weren't interested in the photograph.*

EXERCISE 2

Affix Introduction

a. (Write on the board:)

> **1. real + ly =**
> **2. quick + ly =**
> **3. wide + ly =**

- All these words have the morphograph **ly.**

b. Number your paper from 1 to 3. ✔

c. Add the morphographs together to make new words. Write just the new words. ✔

d. Check your work. Make an **X** next to any word you got wrong.

e. Word 1. Spell **really.** Get ready. (Tap for each letter.) *R-E-A-L-L-Y.*
- (Repeat for: **2. quickly, 3. widely.**)

EXERCISE 3

Spelling Review

a. Get ready to spell words.

b. Word 1 is **rental.**
- What word? (Signal.) *Rental.*
- Spell **rental.** Get ready. (Signal.) *R-E-N-T-A-L.*

c. Word 2 is **unfair.**
- What word? (Signal.) *Unfair.*
- Spell **unfair.** Get ready. (Signal.) *U-N-F-A-I-R.*

d. (Repeat step c for: **3. doubtful, 4. length, 5. swimmer, 6. quoting.**)

e. (Give individual turns on: **1. rental, 2. unfair, 3. doubtful, 4. length, 5. swimmer, 6. quoting.**)

EXERCISE 1

Sentence

a. (Write on the board:)

> **People weren't interested in the photograph.**

- I'll read the sentence on the board: **People weren't interested in the photograph.**
- Let's spell some of those words.
b. Spell **People.** Get ready. (Signal.) *P-E-O-P-L-E.*
- Spell **weren't.** Get ready. (Signal.) *W-E-R-E-N-apostrophe-T.*
- Spell **interested.** Get ready. (Signal.) *I-N-T-E-R-E-S-T-E-D.*
- Spell **photograph.** Get ready. (Signal.) *P-H-O-T-O-G-R-A-P-H.*
c. (Erase the board.)
d. Now let's spell some of the words in that sentence without looking.
- Spell **People.** Get ready. (Signal.) *P-E-O-P-L-E.*
- Spell **weren't.** Get ready. (Signal.) *W-E-R-E-N-apostrophe-T.*
- Spell **interested.** Get ready. (Signal.) *I-N-T-E-R-E-S-T-E-D.*
- Spell **photograph.** Get ready. (Signal.) *P-H-O-T-O-G-R-A-P-H.*

EXERCISE 2

Word Introduction

a. (Write on the board:)

> crease
> press
> chain
> quest
> shirt

b. Get ready to read these words.
- First word: **crease.** What word? (Signal.) *Crease.*
c. Next word: **press.** What word? (Signal.) *Press.*
- (Repeat for: **chain, quest, shirt.**)
d. Now spell those words.
- Spell **crease.** Get ready. (Signal.) *C-R-E-A-S-E.*

e. Spell **press.** Get ready. (Signal.) *P-R-E-S-S.*
- (Repeat for: **chain, quest, shirt.**)
f. (Erase the board.)
- Spell the words without looking.
g. Spell **crease.** Get ready. (Signal.) *C-R-E-A-S-E.*
h. Spell **press.** Get ready. (Signal.) *P-R-E-S-S.*
- (Repeat for: **chain, quest, shirt.**)
i. Get ready to write those words.
j. First word: **crease.** Write it. ✔
- (Repeat for: **press, chain, quest, shirt.**)

EXERCISE 3

Prompted Review

a. (Write on the board:)

> **1. hopefully**
> **2. loosely**
> **3. painfullest**
> **4. madly**
> **5. riding**
> **6. weaker**

b. Word 1 is **hopefully.** Spell **hopefully.** Get ready. (Signal.) *H-O-P-E-F-U-L-L-Y.*
c. Word 2 is **loosely.** Spell **loosely.** Get ready. (Signal.) *L-O-O-S-E-L-Y.*
d. (Repeat step c for: **3. painfullest, 4. madly, 5. riding, 6. weaker.**)
e. (Erase the board.)
- Now spell those words without looking.
f. Word 1 is **hopefully.** Spell **hopefully.** Get ready. (Signal.) *H-O-P-E-F-U-L-L-Y.*
g. Word 2 is **loosely.** Spell **loosely.** Get ready. (Signal.) *L-O-O-S-E-L-Y.*
h. (Repeat step g for: **3. painfullest, 4. madly, 5. riding, 6. weaker.**)
i. (Give individual turns on: **1. hopefully, 2. loosely, 3. painfullest, 4. madly, 5. riding, 6. weaker.**)

Sentence

a. (Write on the board:)

> **People weren't interested in the photograph.**

*   I'll read the sentence on the board: **People weren't interested in the photograph.**
*   Let's spell some of those words.
b. Spell **People.** Get ready. (Signal.)
    P-E-O-P-L-E.
*   Spell **weren't.** Get ready. (Signal.)
    W-E-R-E-N-apostrophe-T.
*   Spell **interested.** Get ready. (Signal.)
    I-N-T-E-R-E-S-T-E-D.
*   Spell **photograph.** Get ready. (Signal.)
    P-H-O-T-O-G-R-A-P-H.
c. (Erase the board.)
d. Now let's spell some of the words in that sentence without looking.
*   Spell **People.** Get ready. (Signal.)
    P-E-O-P-L-E.
*   Spell **weren't.** Get ready. (Signal.)
    W-E-R-E-N-apostrophe-T.
*   Spell **interested.** Get ready. (Signal.)
    I-N-T-E-R-E-S-T-E-D.
*   Spell **photograph.** Get ready. (Signal.)
    P-H-O-T-O-G-R-A-P-H.

Consonant-and-Y Rule

a. (Write on the board:)

> fancy + ly =
> fancy + est =
> fancy + ing =

b. When we add a morphograph to a word that ends with **consonant-and-y,** we sometimes have to change the spelling of that word.
c. Here is the rule: Change the **y** to **i** when you add a morphograph beginning with *anything,* except **i.**
d. My turn: When do you change the **y** to **i?** When the next morphograph begins with anything, except **i.**

e. Your turn: When do you change the **y** to **i?** (Signal.) *When the next morphograph begins with anything, except i.*
f. That's right, when the next morphograph begins with anything, except **i.**
g. (Point to **fancy + ly** on the board:)
*   Does **fancy** end with **consonant-and-y?** (Signal.) *Yes.*
h. The morphograph **ly** does not begin with **i,** so you have to change the **y** to **i.**
i. (Write to show:)

> fancy + ly = fancily
> fancy + est =
> fancy + ing =

j. (Point to **fancy + est** on the board:)
*   Does **fancy** end with **consonant-and-y?** (Signal.) *Yes.*
k. The morphograph **est** does not begin with **i,** so you have to change the **y** to **i.**
l. (Write to show:)

> fancy + ly = fancily
>
> fancy + est = fanciest
>
> fancy + ing =

m. (Point to **fancy + ing** on the board:)
*   Does **fancy** end with **consonant-and-y?** (Signal.) *Yes.*
n. The morphograph **ing** *does* begin with **i,** so you don't change the **y** to **i.**
o. (Write to show:)

> fancy + ly = fancily
>
> fancy + est = fanciest
>
> fancy + ing = fancying

p. Everyone, spell **fancily.** (Tap for each letter.) *F-A-N-C-I-L-Y.*
q. Spell **fanciest.** Get ready. (Tap for each letter.) *F-A-N-C-I-E-S-T.*
r. Spell **fancying.** Get ready. (Tap for each letter.) *F-A-N-C-Y-I-N-G.*

Prompted Review

a. (Write on the board:)

> **1. toughness**
> **2. denial**
> **3. dropper**
> **4. storage**
> **5. smoothly**
> **6. global**

b. Word 1 is **toughness.** Spell **toughness.**
   Get ready. (Signal.) *T-O-U-G-H-N-E-S-S.*

c. Word 2 is **denial.** Spell **denial.** Get ready.
   (Signal.) *D-E-N-I-A-L.*

d. (Repeat step c for: **3. dropper, 4. storage,
   5. smoothly, 6. global.**)

e. (Erase the board.)

• Now write those words without looking.

f. Word 1 is **toughness.** Write **toughness.** ✔

g. Word 2 is **denial.** Write **denial.** ✔

h. (Repeat step g for: **3. dropper, 4. storage,
   5. smoothly, 6. global.**)

i. (Check and correct.)

LESSON 19

EXERCISE 1

Sentence

a. You're going to write this sentence: **People weren't interested in the photograph.**

b. Say the sentence. Get ready. (Signal.) *People weren't interested in the photograph.*

c. Write the sentence. ✔

d. (Write on the board:)

> **People weren't interested in the photograph.**

e. Check your work. Make an **X** next to any word you got wrong. ✔

EXERCISE 2

Consonant-and-Y Rule

a. (Write on the board:)

> **pity + ful =**
>
> **pity + ing =**
>
> **pity + ed =**

b. When we add a morphograph to a word that ends with **consonant-and-y,** we sometimes have to change the spelling of that word.

c. Here is the rule: Change the **y** to **i** when you add a morphograph beginning with *anything,* except **i.**

d. My turn: When do you change the **y** to **i?** When the next morphograph begins with anything, except **i.**

e. Your turn: When do you change the **y** to **i?** (Signal.) *When the next morphograph begins with anything, except **i.***

f. That's right, when the next morphograph begins with anything, except **i.**

g. (Point to **pity + ful** on the board:)
• Does **pity** end with **consonant-and-y?** (Signal.) *Yes.*

h. The morphograph **ful** does not begin with **i,** so you have to change the **y** to **i.**

i. (Write to show:)

> **pity + ful = pitiful**
>
> **pity + ing =**
>
> **pity + ed =**

j. (Point to **pity + ing** on the board:)
• Does **pity** end with **consonant-and-y?** (Signal.) *Yes.*

k. The morphograph **ing** does begin with **i,** so you don't have to change the **y** to **i.**

l. (Write to show:)

> **pity + ful = pitiful**
>
> **pity + ing = pitying**
>
> **pity + ed =**

m. (Point to **pity + ed** on the board:)
• Does **pity** end with **consonant-and-y?** (Signal.) *Yes.*

n. The morphograph **e-d** does not begin with **i,** so you change the **y** to **i.**

o. (Write to show:)

> **pity + ful = pitiful**
>
> **pity + ing = pitying**
>
> **pity + ed = pitied**

p. Everyone, spell **pitiful.** (Tap for each letter.) *P-I-T-I-F-U-L.*

q. Spell **pitying.** Get ready. (Tap for each letter.) *P-I-T-Y-I-N-G.*

r. Spell **pitied.** Get ready. (Tap for each letter.) *P-I-T-I-E-D.*

Spelling Review

a. Get ready to spell words.

b. Word 1 is **lighter.**

- What word? (Signal.) *Lighter.*
- Spell **lighter.** Get ready. (Signal.)
  L-I-G-H-T-E-R.

c. Word 2 is **widely.**

- What word? (Signal.) *Widely.*
- Spell **widely.** Get ready. (Signal.)
  W-I-D-E-L-Y.

d. (Repeat step c for: **3. formal, 4. slipping.**)

e. (Give individual turns on: **1. lighter, 2. widely, 3. formal, 4. slipping.**)

EXERCISE 1

Test

a. Today you have a spelling test. Number your lined paper from 1 through 10. ✔
b. Word 1 is **stretching.** What word? (Signal.) *Stretching.*
• Write the word **stretching.** ✔
c. Word 2 is **incurable.** What word? (Signal.) *Incurable.*
• Write the word **incurable.** ✔
d. Word 3 is **starring.** What word? (Signal.) *Starring.*
• Write the word **starring.** ✔
e. Word 4 is **madness.** What word? (Signal.) *Madness.*
• Write the word **madness.** ✔
f. Word 5 is **weakest.** What word? (Signal.) *Weakest.*
• Write the word **weakest.** ✔
g. Word 6 is **strength.** What word? (Signal.) *Strength.*
• Write the word **strength.** ✔
h. Word 7 is **fashionable.** What word? (Signal.) *Fashionable.*
• Write the word **fashionable.** ✔

i. Word 8 is **formally.** What word? (Signal.) *Formally.*
• Write the word **formally.** ✔
j. Word 9 is **fitness.** What word? (Signal.) *Fitness.*
• Write the word **fitness.** ✔
k. Word 10 is **misspell.** What word? (Signal.) *Misspell.*
• Write the word **misspell.** ✔
i. Pick up your red pen. ✔
Make an **X** next to any word you spelled wrong.
• (Write on the board:)

1. stretching	6. strength
2. incurable	7. fashionable
3. starring	8. formally
4. madness	9. fitness
5. weakest	10. misspell

• Write the correct spelling next to any word you spelled wrong.
(Observe students and give feedback.)

EXERCISE 1

Affix Introduction

a. (Write on the board:)

> **1. de + light =**
> **2. de + press =**
> **3. de + scribe =**

- All these words have the morphograph **de.**
b. Number your paper from 1 to 3. ✔
c. Add the morphographs together to make new words. Write just the new words. ✔
d. Check your work. Make an **X** next to any word you got wrong.
e. Word 1. Spell **delight.** Get ready. (Tap for each letter.) *D-E-L-I-G-H-T.*
- (Repeat for: **2. depress, 3. describe.**)

EXERCISE 2

Consonant-and-Y Rule

a. (Write on the board:)

> **1. heavy + est =**
> **2. lonely + ness =**
> **3. carry + ing =**
> **4. copy + es =**
> **5. deny + al =**
> **6. fancy + ful =**

b. Number your paper from 1 through 6. ✔
- Each of these words ends **consonant-and-y.**
  Copy the board on your paper with the plus and equal signs. ✔
c. Remember, when we add a morphograph to a word that ends **consonant-and-y,** we usually have to change the spelling of that word.
- Here is the rule: Change the **y** to **i** when the next morphograph begins with anything, except **i.**
d. (Point to **est** on the board:)
- Does this suffix begin with an **i?** (Signal.) *No.*
e. The morphograph **est** does not begin with **i,** so we have to change the **y** to **i.**
f. Write **heaviest** after the equal sign for word 1. ✔

- (Write to show:)

> **heavy + est = heaviest**

g. Finish the words on your own. ✔
h. Check your work. Make an **X** next to any word you got wrong.
i. Word 1. Spell **heaviest.** Get ready. (Tap for each letter.) *H-E-A-V-I-E-S-T.*
- (Repeat for: **2. loneliness, 3. carrying, 4. copies, 5. denial, 6. fanciful.**)

EXERCISE 3

Prompted Review

a. (Write on the board:)

> **1. interesting**
> **2. people**
> **3. really**
> **4. decreasing**
> **5. workable**
> **6. namely**

b. Word 1 is **interesting.** Spell **interesting.** Get ready. (Signal.) *I-N-T-E-R-E-S-T-I-N-G.*
c. Word 2 is **people.** Spell **people.** Get ready. (Signal.) *P-E-O-P-L-E.*
d. (Repeat step c for: **3. really, 4. decreasing, 5. workable, 6. namely.**)
e. (Erase the board.)
- Now spell those words without looking.
f. Word 1 is **interesting.** Spell **interesting.** Get ready. (Signal.) *I-N-T-E-R-E-S-T-I-N-G.*
g. Word 2 is **people.** Spell **people.** Get ready. (Signal.) *P-E-O-P-L-E.*
h. (Repeat step g for: **3. really, 4. decreasing, 5. workable, 6. namely.**)
i. (Give individual turns on: **1. interesting, 2. people, 3. really, 4. decreasing, 5. workable, 6. namely.**)

LESSON 22

EXERCISE 1

Affix Introduction

a. (Write on the board:)

> 1. length + en =
> 2. light + en =
> 3. loose + en =

- All these words have the morphograph **e-n.**
b. Number your paper from 1 to 3. ✔
c. Add the morphographs together to make new words. Write just the new words. ✔
d. Check your work. Make an **X** next to any word you got wrong.
e. Word 1. Spell **lengthen.** Get ready. (Tap for each letter.) *L-E-N-G-T-H-E-N.*
- (Repeat for: **2. lighten, 3. loosen.**)

EXERCISE 2

Consonant-and-Y Rule

a. (Write on the board:)

> 1. vary + ed =
> 2. copy + er =
> 3. try + ed =
> 4. study + ing =
> 5. early + er =
> 6. marry + age =

b. Number your paper from 1 through 6. ✔
- Each of these words ends **consonant-and-y.**
  Copy the board on your paper with the plus and equal signs. ✔
c. Remember, when we add a morphograph to a word that ends **consonant-and-y,** we usually have to change the spelling of that word.
- Here is the rule: Change the **y** to **i** when the next morphograph begins with anything, except **i.**
d. (Point to **ed** on the board:)
- Does this suffix begin with an **i?** (Signal.) *No.*
e. The morphograph **e-d** does not begin with **i,** so we have to change the **y** to **i.**
f. Write **varied** after the equal sign for word 1. ✔

- (Write to show:)

> vary + ed = **varied**

g. Finish the words on your own. ✔
h. Check your work. Make an **X** next to any word you got wrong.
i. Word 1. Spell **varied.** Get ready. (Tap for each letter.) *V-A-R-I-E-D.*
- (Repeat for: **2. copier, 3. tried, 4. studying, 5. earlier, 6. marriage.**)

EXERCISE 3

Spelling Review

a. Get ready to spell words.
b. Word 1 is **wildly.**
- What word? (Signal.) *Wildly.*
- Spell **wildly.** Get ready. (Signal.) *W-I-L-D-L-Y.*
c. Word 2 is **mistaking.**
- What word? (Signal.) *Mistaking.*
- Spell **mistaking.** Get ready. (Signal.) *M-I-S-T-A-K-I-N-G.*
d. (Repeat step c for: **3. snugness, 4. toughest, 5. priceless, 6. depress.**)
e. (Give individual turns on: **1. wildly, 2. mistaking, 3. snugness, 4. toughest, 5. priceless, 6. depress.**)

EXERCISE 1

Affix Introduction

a. (Write on the board:)

> 1. pack + age =
> 2. wreck + age =
> 3. store + age =

- All these words have the morphograph **a-g-e.**
b. Number your paper from 1 to 3. ✔
c. Add the morphographs together to make new words. Write just the new words. ✔
d. Check your work. Make an **X** next to any word you got wrong.
e. Word 1. Spell **package.** Get ready. (Tap for each letter.) *P-A-C-K-A-G-E.*
- (Repeat for: **2. wreckage, 3. storage.**)

EXERCISE 2

Affix Introduction

a. (Write on the board:)

> 1. in + human =
> 2. in + land =
> 3. in + born =

- All these words have the morphograph **i-n.**
b. Number your paper from 1 to 3. ✔
c. Add the morphographs together to make new words. Write just the new words. ✔
d. Check your work. Make an **X** next to any word you got wrong.
e. Word 1. Spell **inhuman.** Get ready. (Tap for each letter.) *I-N-H-U-M-A-N.*
- (Repeat for: **2. inland, 3. inborn.**)

EXERCISE 3

Consonant-and-Y Rule

a. (Write on the board:)

> 1. cry + ing =
>
> 2. play + ful =
>
> 3. speedy + est =
>
> 4. story + es =
>
> 5. stay + ed =
>
> 6. worry + ing =

b. Number your paper from 1 through 6. ✔ Copy the board on your paper with the plus and equal signs. ✔
c. Some of these words follow the rule about changing a **y** to **i.** Do these words on your own. ✔
d. Check your work. Make an **X** next to any word you got wrong.
e. Word 1. Spell **crying.** Get ready. (Tap for each letter.) *C-R-Y-I-N-G.*
- (Repeat for: **2. playful, 3. speediest, 4. stories, 5. stayed, 6. worrying.**)

EXERCISE 4

Spelling Review

a. Get ready to spell words.
b. Word 1 is **thoughtless.**
- What word? (Signal.) *Thoughtless.*
- Spell **thoughtless.** Get ready. (Signal.) *T-H-O-U-G-H-T-L-E-S-S.*
c. Word 2 is **breath.**
- What word? (Signal.) *Breath.*
- Spell **breath.** Get ready. (Signal.) *B-R-E-A-T-H.*
d. (Repeat step c for: **3. doubtful, 4. guiding.**)
e. (Give individual turns on: **1. thoughtless, 2. breath, 3. doubtful, 4. guiding.**)

EXERCISE 1

Affix Introduction

a. (Write on the board:)

> 1. boat + s =
> 2. skill + s =
> 3. rock + s =

- All these words have the morphograph **s.**
b. Number your paper from 1 to 3. ✔
c. Add the morphographs together to make new words. Write just the new words. ✔
d. Check your work. Make an **X** next to any word you got wrong.
e. Word 1. Spell **boats.** Get ready. (Tap for each letter.) *B-O-A-T-S.*
- (Repeat for: **2. skills, 3. rocks.**)

EXERCISE 2

Affix Introduction

a. (Write on the board:)

> 1. con + fine =
> 2. con + form =
> 3. con + serve =

- All these words have the morphograph **con.**
b. Number your paper from 1 to 3. ✔
c. Add the morphographs together to make new words. Write just the new words. ✔
d. Check your work. Make an **X** next to any word you got wrong.
e. Word 1. Spell **confine.** Get ready. (Tap for each letter.) *C-O-N-F-I-N-E.*
- (Repeat for: **2. conform, 3. conserve.**)

EXERCISE 3

Consonant-and-Y Rule

a. (Write on the board:)

> 1. worry + ed =
>
> 2. baby + es =
>
> 3. early + est =
>
> 4. worry + ing =
>
> 5. worthy + ness =
>
> 6. fly + ing =

b. Number your paper from 1 through 6. ✔ Copy the board on your paper with the plus and equal signs. ✔
c. Some of these words follow the rule about changing a **y** to **i.** Do these words on your own. ✔
d. Check your work. Make an **X** next to any word you got wrong.
e. Word 1. Spell **worried.** Get ready. (Tap for each letter.) *W-O-R-R-I-E-D.*
- (Repeat for: **2. babies, 3. earliest, 4. worrying, 5. worthiness, 6. flying.**)

Prompted Review

a. (Write on the board:)

> **1. storage**
> **2. informally**
> **3. photographs**
> **4. toughest**
> **5. repressed**
> **6. unlikely**

b. Word 1 is **storage.** Spell **storage.** Get ready. (Signal.) *S-T-O-R-A-G-E.*

c. Word 2 is **informally.** Spell **informally.** Get ready. (Signal.) *I-N-F-O-R-M-A-L-L-Y.*

d. (Repeat step c for: **3. photographs, 4. toughest, 5. repressed, 6. unlikely.**)

e. (Erase the board.)

• Now spell those words without looking.

f. Word 1 is **storage.** Spell **storage.** Get ready. (Signal.) *S-T-O-R-A-G-E.*

g. Word 2 is **informally.** Spell **informally.** Get ready. (Signal.) *I-N-F-O-R-M-A-L-L-Y.*

h. (Repeat step g for: **3. photographs, 4. toughest, 5. repressed, 6. unlikely.**)

i. (Give individual turns on: **1. storage, 2. informally, 3. photographs, 4. toughest, 5. repressed, 6. unlikely.**)

LESSON 25

EXERCISE 1

Affix Introduction

a. (Write on the board:)

> 1. speed + y =
> 2. luck + y =
> 3. salt + y =

- All these words have the morphograph **y.**
b. Number your paper from 1 to 3. ✔
c. Add the morphographs together to make new words. Write just the new words. ✔
d. Check your work. Make an **X** next to any word you got wrong.
e. Word 1. Spell **speedy.** Get ready. (Tap for each letter.) *S-P-E-E-D-Y.*
- (Repeat for: **2. lucky, 3. salty.**)

EXERCISE 2

Affix Introduction

a. (Write on the board:)

> 1. ex + press =
> 2. ex + plain =
> 3. ex + change =

- All these words have the morphograph **ex.**
b. Number your paper from 1 to 3. ✔
c. Add the morphographs together to make new words. Write just the new words. ✔
d. Check your work. Make an **X** next to any word you got wrong.
e. Word 1. Spell **express.** Get ready. (Tap for each letter.) *E-X-P-R-E-S-S.*
- (Repeat for: **2. explain, 3. exchange.**)

EXERCISE 3

Word Introduction

a. (Write on the board:)

> straight
> found
> settle
> agree
> claim

b. Get ready to read these words.
- First word: **straight.** What word? (Signal.) *Straight.*
c. Next word: **found.** What word? (Signal.) *Found.*
- (Repeat for: **settle, agree, claim.**)
d. Now spell those words.
- Spell **straight.** Get ready. (Signal.) *S-T-R-A-I-G-H-T.*
e. Spell **found.** Get ready. (Signal.) *F-O-U-N-D.*
- (Repeat for: **settle, agree, claim.**)
f. (Erase the board.)
- Spell the words without looking.
g. Spell **straight.** Get ready. (Signal.) *S-T-R-A-I-G-H-T.*
h. Spell **found.** Get ready. (Signal.) *F-O-U-N-D.*
- (Repeat for: **settle, agree, claim.**)
i. Get ready to write those words.
j. First word: **straight.** Write it. ✔
- (Repeat for: **found, settle, agree, claim.**)

EXERCISE 4

Prompted Review

a. (Write on the board:)

> 1. people
> 2. defined
> 3. freshening
> 4. ripped

b. Word 1 is **people.** Spell **people.** Get ready. (Signal.) *P-E-O-P-L-E.*
c. Word 2 is **defined.** Spell **defined.** Get ready. (Signal.) *D-E-F-I-N-E-D.*
d. (Repeat step c for: **3. freshening, 4. ripped.**)
e. (Erase the board.)
- Now spell those words without looking.
f. Word 1 is **people.** Spell **people.** Get ready. (Signal.) *P-E-O-P-L-E.*
g. Word 2 is **defined.** Spell **defined.** Get ready. (Signal.) *D-E-F-I-N-E-D.*
h. (Repeat step g for: **3. freshening, 4. ripped.**)
i. (Give individual turns on: **1. people, 2. defined, 3. freshening, 4. ripped.**)

EXERCISE 1

Affix Introduction

a. (Write on the board:)

> 1. state + ment =
> 2. treat + ment =
> 3. govern + ment =

- All these words have the morphograph **ment.**
b. Number your paper from 1 to 3. ✔
c. Add the morphographs together to make new words. Write just the new words. ✔
d. Check your work. Make an **X** next to any word you got wrong.
e. Word 1. Spell **statement.** Get ready. (Tap for each letter.) *S-T-A-T-E-M-E-N-T.*
- (Repeat for: **2. treatment, 3. government.**)

EXERCISE 2

Affix Introduction

a. (Write on the board:)

> 1. pro + found =
> 2. pro + claim =
> 3. pro + file =

- All these words have the morphograph **pro.**
b. Number your paper from 1 to 3. ✔
c. Add the morphographs together to make new words. Write just the new words. ✔
d. Check your work. Make an **X** next to any word you got wrong.
e. Word 1. Spell **profound.** Get ready. (Tap for each letter.) *P-R-O-F-O-U-N-D.*
- (Repeat for: **2. proclaim, 3. profile.**)

EXERCISE 3

Word Introduction

a. (Write on the board:)

> prove
> cause
> great
> text
> spirit
> thirst

b. Get ready to read these words.
- First word: **prove.** What word? (Signal.) *Prove.*
c. Next word: **cause.** What word? (Signal.) *Cause.*
- (Repeat for: **great, text, spirit, thirst.**)
d. Now spell those words.
- Spell **prove.** Get ready. (Signal.) *P-R-O-V-E.*
e. Spell **cause.** Get ready. (Signal.) *C-A-U-S-E.*
- (Repeat for: **great, text, spirit, thirst.**)
f. (Erase the board.)
- Spell the words without looking.
g. Spell **prove.** Get ready. (Signal.) *P-R-O-V-E.*
h. Spell **cause.** Get ready. (Signal.) *C-A-U-S-E.*
- (Repeat for: **great, text, spirit, thirst.**)
i. Get ready to write those words.
j. First word: **prove.** Write it. ✔
- (Repeat for: **cause, great, text, spirit, thirst.**)

Word Building

a. You're going to spell some words made up of more than one morphograph.

b. Word 1: **exchange.**
What's the first morphograph in **exchange?** (Signal.) *Ex.*
Next morphograph? (Signal.) *Change.*

c. Spell **exchange.** Get ready. (Signal.)
E-X-C-H-A-N-G-E.

d. Word 2: **conforming.**
What's the first morphograph in **conforming?** (Signal.) *Con.*
Next morphograph? (Signal.) *Form.*
Next morphograph? (Signal.) *Ing.*

e. Spell **conforming.** Get ready. (Signal.)
C-O-N-F-O-R-M-I-N-G.

• (Repeat steps d and e for: **3. inhuman, 4. unlucky, 5. explained, 6. lights.**)

f. (Give individual turns on: **1. exchange, 2. conforming, 3. inhuman, 4. unlucky, 5. explained, 6. lights.**)

EXERCISE 1

W as a Vowel Letter

a. (Write on the board:)

w

b. **W** is usually a consonant letter, but sometimes it's a vowel letter.
c. Here is the rule: If **w** is at the end of a morphograph, then it is a vowel letter.
• Listen again: (Repeat the rule.)
d. (Change the board to show:)

w
1. throw
2. win
3. want
4. yellow
5. show
6. threw

e. Number 1 is **throw.**
• Is the **w** a vowel letter or a consonant letter in the word **throw?** (Signal.) *A vowel letter.*
• How do you know? (Signal.) *It's at the end of a morphograph.*
f. Number 2 is **win.**
• Is the **w** a vowel letter or a consonant letter in the word **win?** (Signal.) *A consonant letter.*
How do you know? (Signal.) *It's not at the end of a morphograph.*
g. Number 3 is **want.**
• Is the **w** a vowel letter or a consonant letter in the word **want?** (Signal.) *A consonant letter.*
• How do you know? (Signal.) *It's not at the end of a morphograph.*
h. (Repeat step g for: **4. yellow, 5. show, 6. threw.**)

EXERCISE 2

Sentence

a. (Write on the board:)

Anybody would rather be healthy instead of wealthy.

• I'll read the sentence on the board: **Anybody would rather be healthy instead of wealthy.**
• Let's spell some of those words.
b. Spell **Anybody.** Get ready. (Signal.) *A-N-Y-B-O-D-Y.*
• Spell **would.** Get ready. (Signal.) *W-O-U-L-D.*
• Spell **healthy.** Get ready. (Signal.) *H-E-A-L-T-H-Y.*
• Spell **instead.** Get ready. (Signal.) *I-N-S-T-E-A-D.*
• Spell **wealthy.** Get ready. (Signal.) *W-E-A-L-T-H-Y.*
c. Copy this sentence on lined paper.
d. (Pause, then check and correct.)
• Read the sentence you just copied. Get ready. (Signal.) *Anybody would rather be healthy instead of wealthy.*

EXERCISE 3

Prompted Review

a. (Write on the board:)

1. thirsty
2. straight
3. stories
4. wreckage
5. conserving
6. striped

b. Word 1 is **thirsty.** Spell **thirsty.** Get ready. (Signal.) *T-H-I-R-S-T-Y.*
c. Word 2 is **straight.** Spell **straight.** Get ready. (Signal.) *S-T-R-A-I-G-H-T.*
d. (Repeat step c for: **3. stories, 4. wreckage, 5. conserving, 6. striped.**)
e. (Erase the board.)
• Now spell those words without looking.
f. Word 1 is **thirsty.** Spell **thirsty.** Get ready. (Signal.) *T-H-I-R-S-T-Y.*
g. Word 2 is **straight.** Spell **straight.** Get ready. (Signal.) *S-T-R-A-I-G-H-T.*
h. (Repeat step g for: **3. stories, 4. wreckage, 5. conserving, 6. striped.**)
i. (Give individual turns on: **1. thirsty, 2. straight, 3. stories, 4. wreckage, 5. conserving, 6. striped.**)

EXERCISE 1

Affix Introduction

a. (Write on the board:)

> **1. act + ive =**
> **2. pass + ive =**
> **3. mass + ive =**

- All these words have the morphograph **i-v-e.**

b. Number your paper from 1 to 3. ✔

c. Add the morphographs together to make new words. Write just the new words. ✔

d. Check your work. Make an **X** next to any word you got wrong.

e. Word 1. Spell **active.** Get ready. (Tap for each letter.) *A-C-T-I-V-E.*

- (Repeat for: **2. passive, 3. massive.**)

EXERCISE 2

Affix Introduction

a. (Write on the board:)

> **1. act + ion =**
> **2. port + ion =**
> **3. pass + ion =**

- All these words have the morphograph **i-o-n.**

b. Number your paper from 1 to 3. ✔

c. Add the morphographs together to make new words. Write just the new words. ✔

d. Check your work. Make an **X** next to any word you got wrong.

e. Word 1. Spell **action.** Get ready. (Tap for each letter.) *A-C-T-I-O-N.*

- (Repeat for: **2. portion, 3. passion.**)

EXERCISE 3

Sentence

a. (Write on the board:)

> **Anybody would rather be healthy instead of wealthy.**

- I'll read the sentence on the board: **Anybody would rather be healthy instead of wealthy.**
- Let's spell some of those words.

b. Spell **Anybody.** Get ready. (Signal.) *A-N-Y-B-O-D-Y.*

- Spell **would.** Get ready. (Signal.) *W-O-U-L-D.*
- Spell **healthy.** Get ready. (Signal.) *H-E-A-L-T-H-Y.*
- Spell **instead.** Get ready. (Signal.) *I-N-S-T-E-A-D.*
- Spell **wealthy.** Get ready. (Signal.) *W-E-A-L-T-H-Y.*

c. (Erase the board.)

d. Now let's spell some of the words in that sentence without looking.

- Spell **Anybody.** Get ready. (Signal.) *A-N-Y-B-O-D-Y.*
- Spell **would.** Get ready. (Signal.) *W-O-U-L-D.*
- Spell **healthy.** Get ready. (Signal.) *H-E-A-L-T-H-Y.*
- Spell **instead.** Get ready. (Signal.) *I-N-S-T-E-A-D.*
- Spell **wealthy.** Get ready. (Signal.) *W-E-A-L-T-H-Y.*

Word Building

a. (Write on the board:)

> **1. photo + graph + s = _____**
> **2. play + ful + ly = _____**
> **3. sign + al = _____**
> **4. re + solve + ed = _____**
> **5. con + strain + ing = _____**
> **6. length + en + ing = _____**
> **7. run + er = _____**

b. You're going to write the words that go in the blanks.

*   Some of these words follow the final **e** rule and some follow the doubling rule.
    Be careful.
*   Number your paper from 1 to 6. ✔
c. Word 1. Write **photographs** on your paper. ✔
d. Do the rest of the words on your own. ✔
e. Check your work. Make an **X** next to any word you got wrong.
f. Word 1. Spell **photographs**. Get ready.
    (Tap for each letter.)
    P-H-O-T-O-G-R-A-P-H-S.
*   (Repeat for: **2. playfully, 3. signal, 4. resolved, 5. constraining, 6. lengthening, 7. runner.**)

LESSON 29

Affix Introduction

a. (Write on the board:)

> 1. text + ure =
> 2. press + ure =
> 3. feat + ure =

- All these words have the morphograph **u-r-e.**
b. Number your paper from 1 to 3. ✔
c. Add the morphographs together to make new words. Write just the new words. ✔
d. Check your work. Make an **X** next to any word you got wrong.
e. Word 1. Spell **texture.** Get ready. (Tap for each letter.) *T-E-X-T-U-R-E.*
- (Repeat for: **2. pressure, 3. feature.**)

Sentence

a. (Write on the board:)

> **Anybody would rather be healthy instead of wealthy.**

- I'll read the sentence on the board: **Anybody would rather be healthy instead of wealthy.**
- Let's spell some of those words.
b. Spell **Anybody.** Get ready. (Signal.) *A-N-Y-B-O-D-Y.*
- Spell **would.** Get ready. (Signal.) *W-O-U-L-D.*
- Spell **healthy.** Get ready. (Signal.) *H-E-A-L-T-H-Y.*
- Spell **instead.** Get ready. (Signal.) *I-N-S-T-E-A-D.*
- Spell **wealthy.** Get ready. (Signal.) *W-E-A-L-T-H-Y.*
c. (Erase the board.)

d. Now let's spell some of the words in that sentence without looking.
- Spell **Anybody.** Get ready. (Signal.) *A-N-Y-B-O-D-Y.*
- Spell **would.** Get ready. (Signal.) *W-O-U-L-D.*
- Spell **healthy.** Get ready. (Signal.) *H-E-A-L-T-H-Y.*
- Spell **instead.** Get ready. (Signal.) *I-N-S-T-E-A-D.*
- Spell **wealthy.** Get ready. (Signal.) *W-E-A-L-T-H-Y.*

Prompted Review

a. (Write on the board:)

> 1. action
> 2. expressive
> 3. reporter
> 4. government
> 5. proportion

b. Word 1 is **action.** Spell **action.** Get ready. (Signal.) *A-C-T-I-O-N.*
c. Word 2 is **expressive.** Spell **expressive.** Get ready. (Signal.) *E-X-P-R-E-S-S-I-V-E.*
d. (Repeat step c for: **3. reporter, 4. government, 5. proportion.**)
e. (Erase the board.)
- Now write those words without looking.
f. Word 1 is **action.** Write **action.** ✔
g. Word 2 is **expressive.** Write **expressive.** ✔
h. (Repeat step g for: **3. reporter, 4. government, 5. proportion.**)
i. (Check and correct.)

EXERCISE 1

Test

a. Today you have a spelling test. Number your lined paper from 1 through 10. ✔

b. Word 1 is **interesting.** What word? (Signal.) *Interesting.*
- Write the word **interesting.** ✔

c. Word 2 is **priceless.** What word? (Signal.) *Priceless.*
- Write the word **priceless.** ✔

d. Word 3 is **studying.** What word? (Signal.) *Studying.*
- Write the word **studying.** ✔

e. Word 4 is **thoughtlessly.** What word? (Signal.) *Thoughtlessly.*
- Write the word **thoughtlessly.** ✔

f. Word 5 is **fanciest.** What word? (Signal.) *Fanciest.*
- Write the word **fanciest.** ✔

g. Word 6 is **strengthening.** What word? (Signal.) *Strengthening.*
- Write the word **strengthening.** ✔

h. Word 7 is **exchanging.** What word? (Signal.) *Exchanging.*
- Write the word **exchanging.** ✔

i. Word 8 is **shopping.** What word? (Signal.) *Shopping.*
- Write the word **shopping.** ✔

j. Word 9 is **people.** What word? (Signal.) *People.*
- Write the word **people.** ✔

k. Word 10 is **informally.** What word? (Signal.) *Informally.*
- Write the word **informally.** ✔

l. Pick up your red pen. ✔
- Make an **X** next to any word you spelled wrong.
- (Write on the board:)

1. **interesting**	6. **strengthening**
2. **priceless**	7. **exchanging**
3. **studying**	8. **shopping**
4. **thoughtlessly**	9. **people**
5. **fanciest**	10. **informally**

- Write the correct spelling next to any word you spelled wrong.
(Observe students and give feedback.)

EXERCISE 1

Affix Introduction

a. (Write on the board:)

> 1. pre + view =
> 2. pre + school =
> 3. pre + serve =

- All these words have the morphograph **pre.**
b. Number your paper from 1 to 3. ✔
c. Add the morphographs together to make new words. Write just the new words. ✔
d. Check your work. Make an **X** next to any word you got wrong.
e. Word 1. Spell **preview.** Get ready. (Tap for each letter.) *P-R-E-V-I-E-W.*
- (Repeat for: **2. preschool, 3. preserve.**)

EXERCISE 2

Sentence

a. You're going to write this sentence:
Anybody would rather be healthy instead of wealthy.
b. Say the sentence. Get ready. (Signal.) *Anybody would rather be healthy instead of wealthy.*
c. Write the sentence. ✔
d. (Write on the board:)

> **Anybody would rather be healthy instead of wealthy.**

e. Check your work. Make an **X** next to any word you got wrong. ✔

EXERCISE 3

Prompted Review

a. (Write on the board:)

> 1. wealthy
> 2. straightest
> 3. action
> 4. thirsty
> 5. massive
> 6. exchange

b. Word 1 is **wealthy.** Spell **wealthy.** Get ready. (Signal.) *W-E-A-L-T-H-Y.*
c. Word 2 is **straightest.** Spell **straightest.** Get ready. (Signal.) *S-T-R-A-I-G-H-T-E-S-T.*
d. (Repeat step c for: **3. action, 4. thirsty, 5. massive, 6. exchange.**)
e. (Erase the board.)
- Now spell those words without looking.
f. Word 1 is **wealthy.** Spell **wealthy.** Get ready. (Signal.) *W-E-A-L-T-H-Y.*
g. Word 2 is **straightest.** Spell **straightest.** Get ready. (Signal.) *S-T-R-A-I-G-H-T-E-S-T.*
h. (Repeat step g for: **3. action, 4. thirsty, 5. massive, 6. exchange.**)
i. (Give individual turns on: **1. wealthy, 2. straightest, 3. action, 4. thirsty, 5. massive, 6. exchange.**)

EXERCISE 1

S and ES

a. (Write on the board:)

s	**z**	**sh**	**ch**

b. If words end in any of these letters or letter combinations, you add **e-s** instead of **s.**

c. Listen: **catch.** What letters does it end in? (Signal.) *C-H.*

• So do you add **s** or **e-s?** (Signal.) *E-S.*

• Yes, the word is **catches.**
You can hear the **e-s.**

d. Listen: **buzz.** What letter does it end in? (Signal.) *Z.*

• So do you add **s** or **e-s?** (Signal.) *E-S.*

• Yes, the word is **buzzes.**
You can hear the **e-s.**

e. Listen: **hat.** What letter does it end in? (Signal.) *T.*

• So do you add **s** or **e-s?** (Signal.) *S.*

• Yes, the word is **hats.**
There is no **e-s** sound at the end.

f. Listen: **dress.** What letter does it end in? (Signal.) *S.*

• So do you add **s** or **e-s?** (Signal.) *E-S.*

• Yes, the word is **dresses.**
You can hear the **e-s.**

g. Listen: **star.** What letter does it end in? (Signal.) *R.*

• So do you add **s** or **e-s?** (Signal.) *S.*

• Yes, the word is **stars.**
There is no **e-s** sound at the end.

h. Listen: **push.** What letters does it end in? (Signal.) *S-H.*

• So do you add **s** or **e-s?** (Signal.) *E-S.*

• Yes, the word is **pushes.**
You can hear the **e-s.**

EXERCISE 2

Nonword Base

a. (Write on the board:)

1. r e p r e s s i v e
2. p r o c l a i m
3. d e f o r m i n g

b. (Point to **repressive.**)

• What word? (Signal.) *Repressive.*

• What's the first morphograph? (Signal.) *Re.*

• Next morphograph? (Signal.) *Press.*

• Next morphograph? (Signal.) *Ive.*

c. Tell me which morphograph in this word could stand alone. (Pause.) Get ready. (Signal.) *Press.*

d. (Point to **proclaim.**)

• What word? (Signal.) *Proclaim.*

• What's the first morphograph? (Signal.) *Pro.*

• Next morphograph? (Signal.) *Claim.*

e. Tell me which morphograph in this word could stand alone. (Pause.) Get ready. (Signal.) *Claim.*

f. (Point to **deforming.**)

• What word? (Signal.) *Deforming.*

• What's the first morphograph? (Signal.) *De.*

• Next morphograph? (Signal.) *Form.*

• Next morphograph? (Signal.) *Ing.*

g. Tell me which morphograph in this word could stand alone. (Pause.) Get ready. (Signal.) *Form.*

h. Some words with more than one morphograph do not contain a morphograph that can stand alone.

• (Erase the morphographs **press, claim,** and **form.** Substitute **cept, gress,** and **tect** to show:)

1. r e **cept** i v e

2. p r o **gress**

3. d e **tect** i n g

i. (Point to **receptive.**)

• What word? (Signal.) *Receptive.*

• Tell me what morphograph in this word could stand alone. (Pause.) Get ready. (Signal.) *None of them.*

j. Which morphograph takes the place of a morphograph that could stand alone? (Signal.) *Cept.*

• Spell **cept.** Get ready. (Signal.) *C-E-P-T.*
Remember, **cept** is a morphograph that cannot stand alone.

k. (Point to **progress**.)
- You can pronounce this word either as **PRO-gress** or **pro-GRESS.**
- Tell me what morphograph in this word could stand alone. (Pause.) Get ready. (Signal.) *None of them.*

l. Which morphograph takes the place of a morphograph that could stand alone? (Signal.) *Gress.*
- Spell **gress.** Get ready. (Signal.) *G-R-E-S-S.*
  Remember, **gress** is a morphograph that cannot stand alone.

m. (Point to **detecting**.)
- What word? (Signal.) *Detecting.*
- Tell me what morphograph in this word could stand alone. (Pause.) Get ready. (Signal.) *None of them.*

n. Which morphograph takes the place of a morphograph that could stand alone? (Signal.) *Tect.*
- Spell **tect.** Get ready. (Signal.) *T-E-C-T.*
  Remember, **tect** is a morphograph that cannot stand alone.

o. Get ready to write some words that have the morphographs **cept**, **gress**, and **tect.**

p. Word 1: **concept.**
   Write it. ✔

q. Word 2: **regressing.**
   Write it. ✔
- (Repeat step q for: **3. protect, 4. deceptive**.)

r. I'll spell each word. Put an **X** next to any word you missed and write that word correctly.
- (Spell each word twice. Write the words on the board as you spell them.)

1. concept	3. protect
2. regressing	4. deceptive

Spelling Review

a. Get ready to spell words.

b. Word 1 is **prolong.**
- What word? (Signal.) *Prolong.*
- Spell **prolong.** Get ready. (Signal.) *P-R-O-L-O-N-G.*

c. Word 2 is **toughness.**
- What word? (Signal.) *Toughness.*
- Spell **toughness.** Get ready. (Signal.) *T-O-U-G-H-N-E-S-S.*

d. (Repeat step c for: **3. people, 4. instead.**)

e. (Give individual turns on: **1. prolong, 2. toughness, 3. people, 4. instead.**)

EXERCISE 1

Affix Introduction

a. (Write on the board:)

> 1. joy + ous =
> 2. fam + ous =
> 3. fury + ous =

- All these words have the morphograph **o-u-s.**
b. Number your paper from 1 to 3. ✔
c. Add the morphographs together to make new words. Write just the new words. ✔
d. Check your work. Make an **X** next to any word you got wrong.
e. Word 1. Spell **joyous.** Get ready. (Tap for each letter.) *J-O-Y-O-U-S.*
- (Repeat for: **2. famous, 3. furious.**)

EXERCISE 2

Nonword Base

a. (Write on the board:)

> **ject**

- One morphograph that cannot stand alone is **ject.**
- What morphograph? (Signal.) *Ject.*
- Spell **ject.** Get ready. (Signal.) *J-E-C-T.*
b. Get ready to spell words that have the morphograph **ject.**
c. First word: **reject.**
- You can pronounce this word either **RE-ject** or **re-JECT.**
- What's the first morphograph in **reject?** (Signal.) *Re.*
- Next morphograph? (Signal.) *Ject.*
- Spell **reject.** Get ready. (Signal.) *R-E-J-E-C-T.*

d. Next word: **injection.**
- What's the first morphograph in **injection?** (Signal.) *In.*
- Next morphograph? (Signal.) *Ject.*
- Next morphograph? (Signal.) *Ion.*
- Spell **injection.** Get ready. (Signal.) *I-N-J-E-C-T-I-O-N.*
e. (For **dejected [de + ject + ed], conjecture [con + ject + ure],** and **project [pro + ject],** have students identify each morphograph and spell each entire word.)

EXERCISE 3

Prompted Review

a. (Write on the board:)

> 1. matches
> 2. rather
> 3. healthy
> 4. settlement
> 5. government
> 6. confining

b. Word 1 is **matches.** Spell **matches.** Get ready. (Signal.) *M-A-T-C-H-E-S.*
c. Word 2 is **rather.** Spell **rather.** Get ready. (Signal.) *R-A-T-H-E-R.*
d. (Repeat step c for: **3. healthy, 4. settlement, 5. government, 6. confining.**)
e. (Erase the board.)
- Now spell those words without looking.
f. Word 1 is **matches.** Spell **matches.** Get ready. (Signal.) *M-A-T-C-H-E-S.*
g. Word 2 is **rather.** Spell **rather.** Get ready. (Signal.) *R-A-T-H-E-R.*
h. (Repeat step g for: **3. healthy, 4. settlement, 5. government, 6. confining.**)
i. (Give individual turns on: **1. matches, 2. rather, 3. healthy, 4. settlement, 5. government, 6. confining.**)

EXERCISE 1

Word Introduction

a. (Write on the board:)

> duty
> danger
> round
> speak
> fury

b. Get ready to read these words.
- First word: **duty.** What word? (Signal.) *Duty.*
c. Next word: **danger.** What word? (Signal.) *Danger.*
- (Repeat for: **round, speak, fury.**)
d. Now spell those words.
- Spell **duty.** Get ready. (Signal.) *D-U-T-Y.*
e. Spell **danger.** Get ready. (Signal.) *D-A-N-G-E-R.*
- (Repeat for: **round, speak, fury.**)
f. (Erase the board.)
- Spell the words without looking.
g. Spell **duty.** Get ready. (Signal.) *D-U-T-Y.*
h. Spell **danger.** Get ready. (Signal.) *D-A-N-G-E-R.*
- (Repeat for: **round, speak, fury.**)
i. Get ready to write those words.
j. First word: **duty.** Write it. ✔
- (Repeat for: **danger, round, speak, fury.**)

EXERCISE 2

Nonword Base

a. (Write on the board:)

> tect

- One morphograph that cannot stand alone is **tect.**
- What morphograph? (Signal.) *Tect.*
- Spell **tect.** Get ready. (Signal.) *T-E-C-T.*
b. Get ready to spell words that have the morphograph **tect.**
c. First word: **protect.**
- What's the first morphograph in **protect?** (Signal.) *Pro.*
- Next morphograph? (Signal.) *Tect.*
- Spell **protect.** Get ready. (Signal.) *P-R-O-T-E-C-T.*

d. Next word: **detect.**
- What's the first morphograph in **detect?** (Signal.) *De.*
- Next morphograph? (Signal.) *Tect.*
- Spell **detect.** Get ready. (Signal.) *D-E-T-E-C-T.*
e. (For **protection** and **detective,** have students identify each morphograph and spell each entire word.)

EXERCISE 3

Prompted Review

a. (Write on the board:)

> 1. various
> 2. preserving
> 3. toughening
> 4. thirstiness
> 5. misshapened
> 6. interested

b. Word 1 is **various.** Spell **various.** Get ready. (Signal.) *V-A-R-I-O-U-S.*
c. Word 2 is **preserving.** Spell **preserving.** Get ready. (Signal.) *P-R-E-S-E-R-V-I-N-G.*
d. (Repeat step c for: **3. toughening, 4. thirstiness, 5. misshapened, 6. interested.**)
e. (Erase the board.)
- Now spell those words without looking.
f. Word 1 is **various.** Spell **various.** Get ready. (Signal.) *V-A-R-I-O-U-S.*
g. Word 2 is **preserving.** Spell **preserving.** Get ready. (Signal.) *P-R-E-S-E-R-V-I-N-G.*
h. (Repeat step g for: **3. toughening, 4. thirstiness, 5. misshapened, 6. interested.**)
i. (Give individual turns on: **1. various, 2. preserving, 3. toughening, 4. thirstiness, 5. misshapened, 6. interested.**)

EXERCISE 1

S and ES

a. (Write on the board:)

> 1. study + es = studies
> 2. try + es = tries
> 3. carry + es = carries
> 4. worry + es = worries

b. When a word ends **consonant-and-y,** you change the **y** to **i** and add **e-s,** not **s.**

c. Word 1. Spell **studies.** Get ready. (Signal.) *S-T-U-D-I-E-S.*

d. Word 2. Spell **tries.** Get ready. (Signal.) *T-R-I-E-S.*

e. Word 3. Spell **carries.** Get ready. (Signal.) *C-A-R-R-I-E-S.*

f. Word 4. Spell **worries.** Get ready. (Signal.) *W-O-R-R-I-E-S.*

g. Remember, just use your **y-to-i** rule, and add **e-s,** not **s.**

EXERCISE 2

Nonword Base

a. (Write on the board:)

> **gress**

- One morphograph that cannot stand alone is **gress.**
- What morphograph? (Signal.) *Gress.*
- Spell **gress.** Get ready. (Signal.) *G-R-E-S-S.*

b. Get ready to spell words that have the morphograph **gress.**

c. First word: **progress.**
- What's the first morphograph in **progress?** (Signal.) *Pro.*
- Next morphograph? (Signal.) *Gress.*
- Spell **progress.** Get ready. (Signal.) *P-R-O-G-R-E-S-S.*

d. Next word: **progressive.**
- What's the first morphograph in **progressive?** (Signal.) *Pro.*
- Next morphograph? (Signal.) *Gress.*
- Next morphograph? (Signal.) *Ive.*
- Spell **progressive.** Get ready. (Signal.) *P-R-O-G-R-E-S-S-I-V-E.*

e. (For **regress** and **progression,** have students identify each morphograph and spell each entire word.)

EXERCISE 3

Spelling Review

a. Get ready to spell and write some words.

b. Word 1 is **detect.**
- What word? (Signal.) *Detect.*
- Spell **detect.** Get ready. (Signal.) *D-E-T-E-C-T.*
- Write it. ✔

c. Word 2 is **danger.**
- What word? (Signal.) *Danger.*
- Spell danger. Get ready. (Signal.) *D-A-N-G-E-R.*
- Write it. ✔

d. (Repeat step c for: **3. spirit, 4. agree, 5. project, 6. people.**)

e. I'll spell each word.
- Put an **X** next to any word you missed and write that word correctly.
- (Spell each word twice. Write the words on the board as you spell them.)

> | 1. | detect | 4. | agree |
> |----|--------|----|-------|
> | 2. | danger | 5. | project |
> | 3. | spirit | 6. | people |

LESSON 36

EXERCISE 1

Sentence

a. (Write on the board:)

> **The union of physical science and logic was a major development.**

- I'll read the sentence on the board: **The union of physical science and logic was a major development.**
- Let's spell some of those words.

b. Spell **union.** Get ready. (Signal.) *U-N-I-O-N.*
- Spell **physical.** Get ready. (Signal.) *P-H-Y-S-I-C-A-L.*
- Spell **science.** Get ready. (Signal.) *S-C-I-E-N-C-E.*
- Spell **development.** Get ready. (Signal.) *D-E-V-E-L-O-P-M-E-N-T.*

c. Copy this sentence on lined paper.

d. (Pause, then check and correct.)
- Read the sentence you just copied. Get ready. (Signal.) *The union of physical science and logic was a major development.*

EXERCISE 2

Vowel Patterns

a. (Write on the board:)

an en in on un	
Part A	
badge	page
dodge	huge
Part B	
back	mask
thick	think
Part C	
dress	fence
bliss	ice
Part D	
latch	teach
switch	inch

b. The word parts at the top have short vowels.
- The word parts are **an, en, in, on, un.**

c. Part A shows how most short words that end with the sound /j/ work.
- If the word ends with the sounds **adge, edge, idge, odge,** or **udge,** the sound /j/ is spelled **d-g-e.**
- If the word has any other ending, the sound /j/ is usually spelled **g-e.**

d. Part B shows how most short words that end with the sound /k/ work.
- If the word ends with the sounds **ack, eck, ick, ock,** or **uck,** the sound /k/ is spelled **c-k.**
- If the word has any other ending, the sound /k/ is usually spelled **k.**

e. Part C shows how most short words that end with the sound /sss/ work.
- If the word has a short vowel sound followed by the sound /sss/, the sound /sss/ is spelled **s-s.**
- If the word has any other ending, the sound /sss/ is usually spelled **c-e.**

f. Part D shows how most short words that end with the sound /ch/ work.
- If the word has a short vowel sound followed by the sound /ch/, the sound /ch/ is spelled **t-c-h.**
- If the word has any other ending, the sound /ch/ is usually spelled **c-h.**

g. Look over the list and get ready to spell some similar words.
  (Allow students about a half minute.)
- Tell me how to spell **black.** (Pause.) Get ready. (Signal.) *B-L-A-C-K.*

h. Tell me how to spell **reach.** (Pause.) Get ready. (Signal.) *R-E-A-C-H.*
- (Repeat step h for: **fence, judge, rock, pinch, stress, pitch, large, trick.**)

EXERCISE 1

Sentence

a. (Write on the board:)

> **The union of physical science and logic was a major development.**

- I'll read the sentence on the board: **The union of physical science and logic was a major development.**
- Let's spell some of those words.

b. Spell **union.** Get ready. (Signal.) *U-N-I-O-N.*
- Spell **physical.** Get ready. (Signal.) *P-H-Y-S-I-C-A-L.*
- Spell **science.** Get ready. (Signal.) *S-C-I-E-N-C-E.*
- Spell **development.** Get ready. (Signal.) *D-E-V-E-L-O-P-M-E-N-T.*

c. (Erase the board.)

d. Now let's spell some of the words in that sentence without looking.
- Spell **union.** Get ready. (Signal.) *U-N-I-O-N.*
- Spell **physical.** Get ready. (Signal.) *P-H-Y-S-I-C-A-L.*
- Spell **science.** Get ready. (Signal.) *S-C-I-E-N-C-E.*
- Spell **development.** Get ready. (Signal.) *D-E-V-E-L-O-P-M-E-N-T.*

EXERCISE 2

Nonword Base

a. (Write on the board:)

> **cept**

- One morphograph that cannot stand alone is **cept.**
- What morphograph? (Signal.) *Cept.*
- Spell **cept.** Get ready. (Signal.) *C-E-P-T.*

b. Get ready to spell words that have the morphograph **cept.**

c. First word: **concept.**
- What's the first morphograph in **concept?** (Signal.) *Con.*
- Next morphograph? (Signal.) *Cept.*
- Spell **concept.** Get ready. (Signal.) *C-O-N-C-E-P-T.*

d. Next word: **except.**
- What's the first morphograph in **except?** (Signal.) *Ex.*
- Next morphograph? (Signal.) *Cept.*
- Spell **except.** Get ready. (Signal.) *E-X-C-E-P-T.*

e. (For **receptive** and **deception,** have students identify each morphograph and spell each entire word.)

EXERCISE 3

Word Building

a. (Write on the board:)

> 1. catch + es = _____
> 2. back + ing = _____
> 3. huge + ly = _____
> 4. bliss + ful + ly = _____
> 5. pro + tect + ion = _____
> 6. fury + ous + ly = _____

b. You're going to write the words that go in the blanks.
- Some of these words follow the **y**-to-**i** rule. Be careful.
- Number your paper from 1 to 6. ✔

c. Word 1. Write **catches** on your paper. ✔

d. Do the rest of the words on your own. ✔

e. Check your work. Make an **X** next to any word you got wrong.

f. Word 1. Spell **catches.** Get ready. (Tap for each letter.) *C-A-T-C-H-E-S.*
- (Repeat for: **2. backing, 3. hugely, 4. blissfully, 5. protection, 6. furiously.**)

EXERCISE 1

Sentence

a. (Write on the board:)

> **The union of physical science and logic was a major development.**

- I'll read the sentence on the board: **The union of physical science and logic was a major development.**
- Let's spell some of those words.
b. Spell **union.** Get ready. (Signal.) *U-N-I-O-N.*
- Spell **physical.** Get ready. (Signal.) *P-H-Y-S-I-C-A-L.*
- Spell **science.** Get ready. (Signal.) *S-C-I-E-N-C-E.*
- Spell **development.** Get ready. (Signal.) *D-E-V-E-L-O-P-M-E-N-T.*
c. (Erase the board.)
d. Now let's spell some of the words in that sentence without looking.
- Spell **union.** Get ready. (Signal.) *U-N-I-O-N.*
- Spell **physical.** Get ready. (Signal.) *P-H-Y-S-I-C-A-L.*
- Spell **science.** Get ready. (Signal.) *S-C-I-E-N-C-E.*
- Spell **development.** Get ready. (Signal.) *D-E-V-E-L-O-P-M-E-N-T.*

EXERCISE 2

Nonword Base

a. (Write on the board:)

> **tain**

- One morphograph that cannot stand alone is **tain.**
- What morphograph? (Signal.) *Tain.*
- Spell **tain.** Get ready. (Signal.) *T-A-I-N.*
b. Get ready to spell words that have the morphograph **tain.**
c. First word: **contain.**
- What's the first morphograph in **contain?** (Signal.) *Con.*
- Next morphograph? (Signal.) *Tain.*
- Spell **contain.** Get ready. (Signal.) *C-O-N-T-A-I-N.*
d. Next word: **retain.**
- What's the first morphograph in **retain?** (Signal.) *Re.*
- Next morphograph? (Signal.) *Tain.*

- Spell **retain.** Get ready. (Signal.) *R-E-T-A-I-N.*
e. (For **detain** and **maintain,** have students identify each morphograph and spell each entire word.)

EXERCISE 3

Morphographic Analysis

a. (Write on the board:)

> 1. progress =
> 2. detective =
> 3. preschool =
> 4. injection =
> 5. except =
> 6. rejected =

- Copy the board. ✔
- These words are made up of more than one morphograph. You're going to write the morphographs in each word, after the equal sign.
b. **Progress.** What's the first morphograph in **progress?** (Signal.) *Pro.*
c. Write **pro** and a plus sign after the equal sign. ✔
d. What's the next morphograph in **progress?** (Signal.) *Gress.*
e. Write **gress.** ✔
f. Your paper should look like this:
- (Change the board to show:)

> 1. progress = pro + gress
> 2. detective =
> 3. preschool =
> 4. injection =
> 5. except =
> 6. rejected =

g. Do the rest of the words on your own. ✔
- (Change the board to show:)

> 1. progress = pro + gress
> 2. detective = de + tect + ive
> 3. preschool = pre + school
> 4. injection = in + ject + ion
> 5. except = ex + cept
> 6. rejected = re + ject + ed

h. Check your work. Make an **X** next to any word you got wrong.

EXERCISE 1

Sentence

a. You're going to write this sentence: **The union of physical science and logic was a major development.**

b. Say the sentence. Get ready. (Signal.) *The union of physical science and logic was a major development.*

c. Write the sentence. ✔

d. (Write on the board:)

> **The union of physical science and logic was a major development.**

e. Check your work. Make an **X** next to any word you got wrong. ✔

EXERCISE 2

Nonword Base

a. (Write on the board:)

> **spect**

- One morphograph that cannot stand alone is **spect.**
- What morphograph? (Signal.) *Spect.*
- Spell **spect.** Get ready. (Signal.) *S-P-E-C-T.*

b. Get ready to spell words that have the morphograph **spect.**

c. First word: **inspect.**

- What's the first morphograph in **inspect?** (Signal.) *In.*
- Next morphograph? (Signal.) *Spect.*
- Spell **inspect.** Get ready. (Signal.) *I-N-S-P-E-C-T.*

d. Next word: **respectful.**

- What's the first morphograph in **respectful?** (Signal.) *Re.*
- Next morphograph? (Signal.) *Spect.*
- Next morphograph? (Signal.) *Ful.*
- Spell **respectful.** Get ready. (Signal.) *R-E-S-P-E-C-T-F-U-L.*

e. (For **prospect** and **inspection,** have students identify each morphograph and spell each entire word.)

EXERCISE 3

Prompted Review

a. (Write on the board:)

> 1. container
> 2. exception
> 3. progressive
> 4. instead
> 5. helplessness
> 6. usable

b. Word 1 is **container.** Spell **container.** Get ready. (Signal.) *C-O-N-T-A-I-N-E-R.*

c. Word 2 is **exception.** Spell **exception.** Get ready. (Signal.) *E-X-C-E-P-T-I-O-N.*

d. (Repeat step c for: **3. progressive, 4. instead, 5. helplessness, 6. usable.**)

e. (Erase the board.)

- Now spell those words without looking.

f. Word 1 is **container.** Spell **container.** Get ready. (Signal.) *C-O-N-T-A-I-N-E-R.*

g. Word 2 is **exception.** Spell **exception.** Get ready. (Signal.) *E-X-C-E-P-T-I-O-N.*

h. (Repeat step g for: **3. progressive, 4. instead, 5. helplessness, 6. usable.**)

i. (Give individual turns on: **1. container, 2. exception, 3. progressive, 4. instead, 5. helplessness, 6. usable.**)

Test

a. Today you have a spelling test. Number your lined paper from 1 through 10. ✔
b. Word 1 is **various.** What word? (Signal.) *Various.*
- Write the word **various.** ✔
c. Word 2 is **hopped.** What word? (Signal.) *Hopped.*
- Write the word **hopped.** ✔
d. Word 3 is **resolve.** What word? (Signal.) *Resolve.*
- Write the word **resolve.** ✔
e. Word 4 is **reception.** What word? (Signal.) *Reception.*
- Write the word **reception.** ✔
f. Word 5 is **describe.** What word? (Signal.) *Describe.*
- Write the word **describe.** ✔
g. Word 6 is **misspelled.** What word? (Signal.) *Misspelled.*
- Write the word **misspelled.** ✔
h. Word 7 is **unhappiest.** What word? (Signal.) *Unhappiest.*
- Write the word **unhappiest.** ✔

i. Word 8 is **signal.** What word? (Signal.) *Signal.*
- Write the word **signal.** ✔
j. Word 9 is **unfairly.** What word? (Signal.) *Unfairly.*
- Write the word **unfairly.** ✔
k. Word 10 is **government.** What word? (Signal.) *Government.*
- Write the word **government.** ✔
l. Pick up your red pen. ✔
   Make an **X** next to any word you spelled wrong.
- (Write on the board:)

1. various	6. misspelled
2. hopped	7. unhappiest
3. resolve	8. signal
4. reception	9. unfairly
5. describe	10. government

- Write the correct spelling next to any word you spelled wrong.
   (Observe students and give feedback.)

LESSON 41

EXERCISE 1

Affix Introduction

a. (Write on the board:)

> **1. dis + like =**
> **2. dis + arm =**
> **3. dis + ease =**

- All these words have the morphograph **dis.**

b. Number your paper from 1 to 3. ✔

c. Add the morphographs together to make new words. Write just the new words. ✔

d. Check your work. Make an **X** next to any word you got wrong.

e. Word 1. Spell **dislike.** Get ready. (Tap for each letter.) *D-I-S-L-I-K-E.*

- (Repeat for: **2. disarm, 3. disease.**)

EXERCISE 2

Word Building

a. (Write on the board:)

> **1. re + spect + ed = _____**
> **2. re + tain + er = _____**
> **3. re + act + ion = _____**
> **4. pro + ject + ion = _____**
> **5. pre + scribe + ed = _____**
> **6. treat + ment = _____**

b. You're going to write the words that go in the blanks.

- Number your paper from 1 to 6. ✔

c. Word 1. Write **respected** on your paper. ✔

d. Do the rest of the words on your own. ✔

e. Check your work. Make an **X** next to any word you got wrong.

f. Word 1. Spell **respected.** Get ready. (Tap for each letter.) *R-E-S-P-E-C-T-E-D.*

- (Repeat for: **2. retainer, 3. reaction, 4. projection, 5. prescribed, 6. treatment.**)

EXERCISE 3

Vowel Patterns

a. Some words end in a short vowel followed by one more sound.

b. Tell me how the final sound is spelled.

c. Tell me how the sound **/j/** is spelled after a short vowel. (Pause.) Get ready. (Signal.) *D-G-E.*

d. Tell me how the sound **/k/** is spelled after a short vowel. (Pause.) Get ready. (Signal.) *C-K.*

e. Tell me how the sound **/sss/** is spelled after a short vowel. (Pause.) Get ready. (Signal.) *S-S.*

f. Tell me how the sound **/ch/** is spelled after a short vowel. (Pause.) Get ready. (Signal.) *T-C-H.*

g. Get ready to spell some words with those sounds.

h. Spell **pledge.**

- Get ready. (Signal.) *P-L-E-D-G-E.*

- (Repeat step h for: **range, ditch, look, voice, class, thank, stack, ledge.**)

EXERCISE 4

Prompted Review

a. (Write on the board:)

> **1. science**
> **2. people**
> **3. inspection**
> **4. maintained**
> **5. rather**
> **6. interesting**

b. Word 1 is **science.** Spell **science.** Get ready. (Signal.) *S-C-I-E-N-C-E.*

c. Word 2 is **people.** Spell **people.** Get ready. (Signal.) *P-E-O-P-L-E.*

d. (Repeat step c for: **3. inspection, 4. maintained, 5. rather, 6. interesting.**)

e. (Erase the board.)

- Now spell those words without looking.

f. Word 1 is **science.** Spell **science.** Get ready. (Signal.) *S-C-I-E-N-C-E.*

g. Word 2 is **people.** Spell **people.** Get ready. (Signal.) *P-E-O-P-L-E.*

h. (Repeat step g for: **3. inspection, 4. maintained, 5. rather, 6. interesting.**)

i. (Give individual turns on: **1. science, 2. people, 3. inspection, 4. maintained, 5. rather, 6. interesting.**)

LESSON 42

EXERCISE 1

Affix Introduction

a. (Write on the board:)

> 1. tour + ist =
> 2. art + ist =
> 3. race + ist =

- All these words have the morphograph **ist.**
b. Number your paper from 1 to 3. ✔
c. Add the morphographs together to make new words. Write just the new words. ✔
d. Check your work. Make an **X** next to any word you got wrong.
e. Word 1. Spell **tourist.** Get ready. (Tap for each letter.) *T-O-U-R-I-S-T.*
- (Repeat for: **2. artist, 3. racist.**)

EXERCISE 2

Morphographic Analysis

a. (Write on the board:)

> 1. usable =
> 2. careless =
> 3. pleasing =
> 4. liked =
> 5. removable =
> 6. building =

- Copy the board. ✔
- These words are made up of more than one morphograph. You're going to write the morphographs in each word, after the equal sign.
b. **Usable.** What's the first morphograph in **usable?** (Signal.) *Use.*
c. Write **use** and a plus sign after the equal sign. ✔
- Don't forget to write the **e** at the end of **use.**
d. What's the next morphograph in **usable?** (Signal.) *Able.*
e. Write **able.** ✔

f. Your paper should look like this:
- (Change the board to show:)

> 1. usable = use + able
> 2. careless =
> 3. pleasing =
> 4. liked =
> 5. removable =
> 6. building =

g. Do the rest of the words on your own. You have to write an **e** at the end of some of the morphographs. ✔
- (Change the board to show:)

> 1. usable = use + able
> 2. careless = care + less
> 3. pleasing = please + ing
> 4. liked = like + ed
> 5. removable = re + move + able
> 6. building = build + ing

h. Check your work. Make an **X** next to any word you got wrong.

EXERCISE 3

Spelling Review

a. You're going to spell words.
b. Word 1 is **projection.**
- What word? (Signal.) *Projection.*
- Spell **projection.** Get ready. (Signal.) *P-R-O-J-E-C-T-I-O-N.*
c. Word 2 is **receptive.** Write it.
- What word? (Signal.) *Receptive.*
- Spell **receptive.** Get ready. (Signal.) *R-E-C-E-P-T-I-V-E.*
d. (Repeat step c for: **3. wealthy, 4. signs, 5. rather, 6. development.**)
e. (Give individual turns on: **1. projection, 2. receptive, 3. wealthy, 4. signs, 5. rather, 6. development.**)

EXERCISE 1

Nonword Base

a. (Write on the board:)

> **pel**

- One morphograph that cannot stand alone is **pel.**
- What morphograph? (Signal.) *Pel.*
- Spell **pel.** Get ready. (Signal.) *P-E-L.*

b. Get ready to spell words that have the morphograph **pel.**

c. First word: **propel.**
- What's the first morphograph in **propel?** (Signal.) *Pro.*
- Next morphograph? (Signal.) *Pel.*
- Spell **propel.** Get ready. (Signal.) *P-R-O-P-E-L.*

d. Next word: **expel.**
- What's the first morphograph in **expel?** (Signal.) *Ex.*
- Next morphograph? (Signal.) *Pel.*
- Spell **expel.** Get ready. (Signal.) *E-X-P-E-L.*

e. (For **dispel** and **repel,** have students identify each morphograph and spell each entire word.)

EXERCISE 2

Word Building

a. (Write on the board:)

> 1. dis + place + ment = _____
> 2. pre + vent + ion = _____
> 3. pack + age + ing = _____
> 4. nerve + ous + ly = _____
> 5. create + ive + ly = _____
> 6. wealth + y = _____

b. You're going to write the words that go in the blanks.
- Number your paper from 1 to 6. ✔

c. Word 1. Write **displacement** on your paper. ✔

d. Do the rest of the words on your own. ✔

e. Check your work. Make an **X** next to any word you got wrong.

f. Word 1. Spell **displacement.** Get ready. (Tap for each letter.) *D-I-S-P-L-A-C-E-M-E-N-T.*
- (Repeat for: **2. prevention, 3. packaging, 4. nervously, 5. creatively, 6. wealthy.**)

EXERCISE 3

Spelling Review

a. Get ready to spell words.

b. Word 1 is **typist.**
- What word? (Signal.) *Typist.*
- Spell **typist.** Get ready. (Signal.) *T-Y-P-I-S-T.*

c. Word 2 is **classic.**
- What word? (Signal.) *Classic.*
- Spell **classic.** Get ready. (Signal.) *C-L-A-S-S-I-C.*

d. (Repeat step c for: **3. faithfully, 4. unfounded, 5. pitiful, 6. hurrying.**)

e. (Give individual turns on: **1. typist, 2. classic, 3. faithfully, 4. unfounded, 5. pitiful, 6. hurrying.**)

EXERCISE 1

Nonword Base

a. (Write on the board:)

> **vise**

- One morphograph that cannot stand alone is **vise.**
- It is usually pronounced **vize.**
- What morphograph? (Signal.) *Vise.*
- Spell **vise.** Get ready. (Signal.) *V-I-S-E.*

b. Get ready to spell words that have the morphograph **vise.**

c. First word: **revise.**
- What's the first morphograph in **revise?** (Signal.) *Re.*
- Next morphograph? (Signal.) *Vise.*
- Spell **revise.** Get ready. (Signal.) *R-E-V-I-S-E.*

d. Next word: **devise.**
- What's the first morphograph in **devise?** (Signal.) *De.*
- Next morphograph? (Signal.) *Vise.*
- Spell **devise.** Get ready. (Signal.) *D-E-V-I-S-E.*

e. (For **vision [vise + ion],** have students identify each morphograph and spell the entire word.)

EXERCISE 2

Morphographic Analysis

a. (Write on the board:)

> 1. **typist =**
> 2. **government =**
> 3. **confining =**
> 4. **reaction =**
> 5. **protection =**
> 6. **photographs =**

- Copy the board. ✔
- Write the morphographs in each word after the equal sign. Put plus signs between the morphographs. ✔

b. (Change the board to show:)

> 1. **typist =** type + ist
> 2. **government =** govern + ment
> 3. **confining =** con + fine + ing
> 4. **reaction =** re + act + ion
> 5. **protection =** pro + tect + ion
> 6. **photographs =** photo + graph + s

c. Check your work. Make an **X** next to any word you got wrong.

EXERCISE 3

Prompted Review

a. (Write on the board:)

> 1. **reaction**
> 2. **diseased**
> 3. **thirstiest**
> 4. **physical**
> 5. **disrespectful**
> 6. **furiously**

b. Word 1 is **reaction.** Spell **reaction.** Get ready. (Signal.) *R-E-A-C-T-I-O-N.*

c. Word 2 is **diseased.** Spell **diseased.** Get ready. (Signal.) *D-I-S-E-A-S-E-D.*

d. (Repeat step c for: **3. thirstiest, 4. physical, 5. disrespectful, 6. furiously.**)

e. (Erase the board.)
- Now spell those words without looking.

f. Word 1 is **reaction.** Spell **reaction.** Get ready. (Signal.) *R-E-A-C-T-I-O-N.*

g. Word 2 is **diseased.** Spell **diseased.** Get ready. (Signal.) *D-I-S-E-A-S-E-D.*

h. (Repeat step g for: **3. thirstiest, 4. physical, 5. disrespectful, 6. furiously.**)

i. (Give individual turns on: **1. reaction, 2. diseased, 3. thirstiest, 4. physical, 5. disrespectful, 6. furiously.**)

LESSON 45

EXERCISE 1

Word Introduction

a. (Write on the board:)

> ready
> build
> bought
> simple
> cross
> chance

b. Get ready to read these words.
- First word: **ready.** What word? (Signal.) *Ready.*
c. Next word: **build.** What word? (Signal.) *Build.*
- (Repeat for: **bought, simple, cross, chance.**)
d. Now spell those words.
- Spell **ready.** Get ready. (Signal.) *R-E-A-D-Y.*
e. Spell **build.** Get ready. (Signal.) *B-U-I-L-D.*
- (Repeat for: **bought, simple, cross, chance.**)
f. (Erase the board.)
- Spell the words without looking.
g. Spell **ready.** Get ready. (Signal.) *R-E-A-D-Y.*
h. Spell **build.** Get ready. (Signal.) *B-U-I-L-D.*
- (Repeat for: **bought, simple, cross, chance.**)
i. Get ready to write those words.
j. First word: **ready.** Write it. ✔
- (Repeat for: **build, bought, simple, cross, chance.**)

EXERCISE 2

Word Building

a. You're going to spell some words made up of more than one morphograph.
b. Word 1: **traction.**
- What's the first morphograph in **traction?** (Signal.) *Tract.*
- Next morphograph? (Signal.) *Ion.*
c. Spell **traction.** Get ready. (Signal.) *T-R-A-C-T-I-O-N.*

d. Word 2: **diseased.**
- What's the first morphograph in **diseased?** (Signal.) *Dis.*
- Next morphograph? (Signal.) *Ease.*
- Next morphograph? (Signal.) *Ed.*
e. Spell **diseased.** Get ready. (Signal.) *D-I-S-E-A-S-E-D.*
- (Repeat steps d and e for: **3. expel, [ex + pel], 4. division, [di + vise +ion], 5. logical, [logic + al], 6. inspection, [in + spect + ion].**)
f. (Give individual turns on: **1. traction, 2. diseased, 3. expel, 4. division, 5. logical, 6. inspection.**)

EXERCISE 3

Sentence Variation

a. Get ready to write on lined paper.
- You are going to write a sentence made up of words you know how to spell. Put the right punctuation mark at the end of the sentence.
b. The sentence is **The people respected the powerful and thoughtful mother.**
- Say that sentence. Get ready. (Signal.) *The people respected the powerful and thoughtful mother.*
- (Repeat until firm.)
c. Write it. ✔
d. Get ready to check your spelling. Put an **X** next to any word you missed.
e. Spell **The.** Get ready. (Signal.) *T-H-E.*
- Check it. ✔
f. Spell **people.** Get ready. (Signal.) *P-E-O-P-L-E.*
- Check it. ✔
g. Spell **respected.** Get ready. (Signal.) *R-E-S-P-E-C-T-E-D.*
- Check it. ✔
- (Repeat for: **the, powerful, and, thoughtful, mother.**)
h. What puctuation mark did you put at the end of the sentence? (Signal.) *A period.*
- Check it. ✔
i. Fix any words you missed.

EXERCISE 1

Affix Introduction

a. (Write on the board:)

> **1. graph + ic =**
> **2. hero + ic =**
> **3. base + ic =**

- All these words have the morphograph **ic.**
b. Number your paper from 1 to 3. ✔
c. Add the morphographs together to make new words. Write just the new words. ✔
d. Check your work. Make an **X** next to any word you got wrong.
e. Word 1. Spell **graphic.** Get ready. (Tap for each letter.) *G-R-A-P-H-I-C.*
- (Repeat for: **2. heroic, 3. basic.**)

EXERCISE 2

Sentence Variation

a. Get ready to write on lined paper.
- You are going to write a sentence made up of words you know how to spell. Put the right punctuation mark at the end of the sentence.
b. The sentence is **A scribe had a profound interest in physical science.**
- Say that sentence. Get ready. (Signal.) *A scribe had a profound interest in physical science.*
- (Repeat until firm.)
c. Write it. ✔
d. Get ready to check your spelling. Put an **X** next to any word you missed.
e. Spell **scribe.** Get ready. (Signal.) *S-C-R-I-B-E.*
- Check it. ✔
f. Spell **had.** Get ready. (Signal.) *H-A-D.*
- Check it. ✔
- (Repeat for: **profound, interest, physical, science.**)
g. What punctuation mark did you put at the end of the sentence? (Signal.) *A period.*
- Check it. ✔
h. Fix any words you missed.

EXERCISE 3

Spelling Review

a. Get ready to spell words.
b. Word 1 is **development.**
- What word? (Signal.) *Development.*
- Spell **development.** Get ready. (Signal.) *D-E-V-E-L-O-P-M-E-N-T.*
c. Word 2 is **traction.**
- What word? (Signal.) *Traction.*
- Spell **traction.** Get ready. (Signal.) *T-R-A-C-T-I-O-N.*
d. (Repeat step c for: **3. government, 4. tourists, 5. protective, 6. venture.**)
e. (Give individual turns on: **1. development, 2. traction, 3. government, 4. tourists, 5. protective, 6. venture.**)

EXERCISE 1

Nonword Base

a. (Write on the board:)

> **duce**

- One morphograph that combines with other morphographs is **duce.**
- What morphograph? (Signal.) *Duce.*
- Spell **duce.** Get ready. (Signal.) *D-U-C-E.*

b. Get ready to spell words that have the morphograph **duce.**

c. First word: **produce.**

- What's the first morphograph in **produce?** (Signal.) *Pro.*
- Next morphograph? (Signal.) *Duce.*
- Spell **produce.** Get ready. (Signal.) *P-R-O-D-U-C-E.*

d. Next word: **reducing.**

- What's the first morphograph in **reducing?** (Signal.) *Re.*
- Next morphograph? (Signal.) *Duce.*
- Next morphograph? (Signal.) *Ing.*
- Spell **reducing.** Get ready. (Signal.) *R-E-D-U-C-I-N-G.*

e. (For **deduce,** have students identify each morphograph and spell the entire word.)

EXERCISE 2

Morphographic Analysis)

a. (Write on the board:)

> 1. winner =
> 2. sadness =
> 3. saddest =
> 4. cutting =
> 5. fitness =
> 6. hopping =

- Copy the board.
- These words are made up of more than one morphograph. You're going to write the morphographs in each word after the equal sign.

b. **Winner.** What's the first morphograph in **winner?** (Signal.) *Win.*

c. Write **win** and a plus sign after the equal sign. ✔

- Don't forget to write just one **n** in **win.**

d. What's the next morphograph in **winner?** (Signal.) *Er.*

e. Write **e-r.** ✔

f. Your paper should look like this:

- (Change the board to show:)

> 1. winner = win + er
> 2. sadness =
> 3. saddest =
> 4. cutting =
> 5. fitness =
> 6. hopping =

g. Do the rest of the words on your own. ✔ You have to change a double letter to a single letter in some of these words.

- (Change the board to show:)

> 1. winner = win + er
> 2. sadness = sad + ness
> 3. saddest = sad + est
> 4. cutting = cut + ing
> 5. fitness = fit + ness
> 6. hopping = hop + ing

h. Check your work. Make an **X** next to any word you got wrong.

EXERCISE 3

Prompted Review

a. (Write on the board:)

> 1. artistic
> 2. rebuilding
> 3. provision
> 4. repel
> 5. dangerously
> 6. fatally

b. Word 1 is **artistic.** Spell **artistic.** Get ready. (Signal.) *A-R-T-I-S-T-I-C.*

c. Word 2 is **rebuilding.** Spell **rebuilding.** Get ready. (Signal.) *R-E-B-U-I-L-D-I-N-G.*

d. (Repeat step c for: **3. provision, 4. repel, 5. dangerously, 6. fatally.**)

e. (Erase the board.)
 • Now spell those words without looking.

f. Word 1 is **artistic.** Spell **artistic.** Get ready. (Signal.) *A-R-T-I-S-T-I-C.*

g. Word 2 is **rebuilding.** Spell **rebuilding.** Get ready. (Signal.) *R-E-B-U-I-L-D-I-N-G.*

h. (Repeat step g for: **3. provision, 4. repel, 5. dangerously, 6. fatally.**)

i. (Give individual turns on: **1. artistic, 2. rebuilding, 3. provision, 4. repel, 5. dangerously, 6. fatally.**)

EXERCISE 1

Word Introduction

a. (Write on the board:)

> chief
> niece
> grief
> brief
> thief

b. Get ready to read these words.
- In each of these words, the sound /ē/ is spelled **i-e.**
- First word: **chief.** What word? (Signal.) *Chief.*
c. Next word: **niece.** What word? (Signal.) *Niece.*
- (Repeat for: **grief, brief, thief.**)
d. Now spell those words.
- Spell **chief.** Get ready. (Signal.) *C-H-I-E-F.*
e. Spell **niece.** Get ready. (Signal.) *N-I-E-C-E.*
- (Repeat for: **grief, brief, thief.**)
f. (Erase the board.)
- Spell the words without looking.
g. Spell **chief.** Get ready. (Signal.) *C-H-I-E-F.*
h. Spell **niece.** Get ready. (Signal.) *N-I-E-C-E.*
- (Repeat for: **grief, brief, thief.**)

EXERCISE 2

Word Building

a. (Write on the board:)

> 1. scene + ic = _____
> 2. in + duce + ing = _____
> 3. simple + y = _____
> 4. re + vise + ion = _____
> 5. in + spect + ion = _____
> 6. worry + es = _____

b. You're going to write the words that go in the blanks.
- Number your paper from 1 to 6. ✔
c. Word 1. Write **scenic** on your paper. ✔
d. Do the rest of the words on your own. ✔
e. Check your work. Make an **X** next to any word you got wrong.
f. Word 1. Spell **scenic.** Get ready. (Tap for each letter.) *S-C-E-N-I-C.*
- (Repeat for: **2. inducing, 3. simply, 4. revision, 5. inspection, 6. worries.**)

EXERCISE 3

Spelling Review

a. Get ready to spell words.
b. Word 1 is **weren't.**
- What word? (Signal.) *Weren't.*
- Spell **weren't.** Get ready. (Signal.) *W-E-R-E-N-apostrophe-T.*
c. Word 2 is **really.**
- What word? (Signal.) *Really.*
- Spell **really.** Get ready. (Signal.) *R-E-A-L-L-Y.*
d. (Repeat step c for: **3. container, 4. healthiest, 5. shipped, 6. trial.**)
e. (Give individual turns on: **1. weren't, 2. really, 3. container, 4. healthiest, 5. shipped, 6. trial.**)

LESSON 49

EXERCISE 1

Word Introduction

a. (Write on the board:)

> grief
> chief
> thief
> niece
> brief

b. In each of these words, the sound /ē/ is spelled **i-e.**
• Spell **grief.** Get ready. (Signal.) *G-R-I-E-F.*
c. Spell **chief.** Get ready. (Signal.) *C-H-I-E-F.*
• (Repeat for: **thief, niece, brief.**)
d. (Erase the board.)
• Spell the words without looking.
e. Spell **grief.** Get ready. (Signal.) *G-R-I-E-F.*
f. Spell **chief.** Get ready. (Signal.) *C-H-I-E-F.*
• (Repeat for: **thief, niece, brief.**)

EXERCISE 2

Word Building

a. (Write on the board:)

> 1. ex + pel = _____
> 2. cube + ic = _____
> 3. style + ist = _____
> 4. de + tain + ed = _____
> 5. act + ive + ly = _____
> 6. dis + prove + en = _____

b. You're going to write the words that go in the blanks.
• Number your paper from 1 to 6. ✔
c. Word 1. Write **expel** on your paper. ✔
d. Do the rest of the words on your own. ✔
e. Check your work. Make an **X** next to any word you got wrong.
f. Word 1. Spell **expel.** Get ready. (Tap for each letter.) *E-X-P-E-L.*
• (Repeat for: **2. cubic, 3. stylist, 4. detained, 5. actively, 6. disproven.**)

EXERCISE 3

Prompted Review

a. (Write on the board:)

> 1. chiefly
> 2. briefest
> 3. scenic
> 4. producing
> 5. rhythmic
> 6. incurable

b. Word 1 is **chiefly.** Spell **chiefly.** Get ready. (Signal.) *C-H-I-E-F-L-Y.*
c. Word 2 is **briefest.** Spell **briefest.** Get ready. (Signal.) *B-R-I-E-F-E-S-T.*
d. (Repeat step c for: **3. scenic, 4. producing, 5. rhythmic, 6. incurable.**)
e. (Erase the board.)
• Now spell those words without looking.
f. Word 1 is **chiefly.** Spell **chiefly.** Get ready. (Signal.) *C-H-I-E-F-L-Y.*
g. Word 2 is **briefest.** Spell **briefest.** Get ready. (Signal.) *B-R-I-E-F-E-S-T.*
h. (Repeat step g for: **3. scenic, 4. producing, 5. rhythmic, 6. incurable.**)
i. (Give individual turns on: **1. chiefly, 2. briefest, 3. scenic, 4. producing, 5. rhythmic, 6. incurable.**)

EXERCISE 1

Test

a. Today you have a spelling test. Number your lined paper from 1 through 10. ✔

b. Word 1 is **unhurried.** What word? (Signal.) *Unhurried.*

• Write the word **unhurried.** ✔

c. Word 2 is **diseases.** What word? (Signal.) *Diseases.*

• Write the word **diseases.** ✔

d. Word 3 is **reception.** What word? (Signal.) *Reception.*

• Write the word **reception.** ✔

e. Word 4 is **artistic.** What word? (Signal.) *Artistic.*

• Write the word **artistic.** ✔

f. Word 5 is **detective.** What word? (Signal.) *Detective.*

• Write the word **detective.** ✔

g. Word 6 is **physical.** What word? (Signal.) *Physical.*

• Write the word **physical.** ✔

h. Word 7 is **instead.** What word? (Signal.) *Instead.*

• Write the word **instead.** ✔

i. Word 8 is **hurrying.** What word? (Signal.) *Hurrying.*

• Write the word **hurrying.** ✔

j. Word 9 is **spotless.** What word? (Signal.) *Spotless.*

• Write the word **spotless.** ✔

k. Word 10 is **carried.** What word? (Signal.) *Carried.*

• Write the word **carried.** ✔

l. Pick up your red pen. ✔
Make an **X** next to any word you spelled wrong.

• (Write on the board:)

1. unhurried	6. physical
2. diseases	7. instead
3. reception	8. hurrying
4. artistic	9. spotless
5. detective	10. carried

• Write the correct spelling next to any word you spelled wrong.
(Observe students and give feedback.)

EXERCISE 1

Affix Introduction

a. (Write on the board:)

> 1. style + ish =
> 2. child + ish =
> 3. fool + ish =

- All these words have the morphograph **ish**.
b. Number your paper from 1 to 3. ✔
c. Add the morphographs together to make new words. Write just the new words. ✔
d. Check your work. Make an **X** next to any word you got wrong.
e. Word 1. Spell **stylish**. Get ready. (Tap for each letter.) *S-T-Y-L-I-S-H.*
- (Repeat for: **2. childish, 3. foolish.**)

EXERCISE 2

Sentence

a. (Write on the board:)

> **The committee had high regard for honesty and courage.**

- I'll read the sentence on the board: **The committee had high regard for honesty and courage.**
- Let's spell some of those words.
b. Spell **committee**. Get ready. (Signal.) *C-O-M-M-I-T-T-E-E.*
- Spell **high**. Get ready. (Signal.) *H-I-G-H.*
- Spell **regard**. Get ready. (Signal.) *R-E-G-A-R-D.*
- Spell **honesty**. Get ready. (Signal.) *H-O-N-E-S-T-Y.*
- Spell **courage**. Get ready. (Signal.) *C-O-U-R-A-G-E.*
c. Copy this sentence on lined paper.
d. (Pause, then check and correct.)
- Read the sentence you just copied. Get ready. (Signal.) *The committee had high regard for honesty and courage.*

EXERCISE 3

Prompted Review

a. (Write on the board:)

> 1. stylist
> 2. revision
> 3. producing
> 4. simply
> 5. artistic
> 6. science

b. Word 1 is **stylist**. Spell **stylist**. Get ready. (Signal.) *S-T-Y-L-I-S-T.*
c. Word 2 is **revision**. Spell **revision**. Get ready. (Signal.) *R-E-V-I-S-I-O-N.*
d. (Repeat step c for: **3. producing, 4. simply, 5. artistic, 6. science.**)
e. (Erase the board.)
- Now spell those words without looking.
f. Word 1 is **stylist**. Spell **stylist**. Get ready. (Signal.) *S-T-Y-L-I-S-T.*
g. Word 2 is **revision**. Spell **revision**. Get ready. (Signal.) *R-E-V-I-S-I-O-N.*
h. (Repeat step g for: **3. producing, 4. simply, 5. artistic, 6. science.**)
i. (Give individual turns on: **1. stylist, 2. revision, 3. producing, 4. simply, 5. artistic, 6. science.**)

EXERCISE 1

Morphographic Analysis

a. (Write on the board:)

> 1. studied =
> 2. flying =
> 3. tried =
> 4. worried =
> 5. copies =
> 6. staying =

- Copy the board. ✔
- These words are made up of more than one morphograph. You're going to write the morphographs in each word after the equal sign.
b. **Studied.** What's the first morphograph in **studied?** (Signal.) *Study.*
c. Write **study** and a plus sign after the equal sign. ✔
- Don't forget to write the **y** at the end of **study.**
d. What's the next morphograph in **studied?** (Signal.) *Ed.*
e. Write **e-d.** ✔
f. Your paper should look like this:
- (Change the board to show:)

> 1 studied = study + ed
> 2. flying =
> 3. tried =
> 4. worried =
> 5. copies =
> 6. staying =

g. Do the rest of the words on your own. ✔ You have to write a **y** at the end of some of the morphographs.
- (Change the board to show:)

> 1. studied = study + ed
> 2. flying = fly + ing
> 3. tried = try + ed
> 4. worried = worry + ed
> 5. copies = copy + es
> 6. staying = stay + ing

h. Check your work. Make an **X** next to any word you got wrong. ✔

EXERCISE 2

Sentence

a. (Write on the board:)

> **The committee had high regard for honesty and courage.**

- I'll read the sentence on the board: **The committee had high regard for honesty and courage.**
- Let's spell some of those words.
b. Spell **committee.** Get ready. (Signal.) *C-O-M-M-I-T-T-E-E.*
- Spell **high.** Get ready. (Signal.) *H-I-G-H.*
- Spell **regard.** Get ready. (Signal.) *R-E-G-A-R-D.*
- Spell **honesty.** Get ready. (Signal.) *H-O-N-E-S-T-Y.*
- Spell **courage.** Get ready. (Signal.) *C-O-U-R-A-G-E.*
c. (Erase the board.)
d. Now let's spell some of the words in that sentence without looking.
- Spell **committee.** Get ready. (Signal.) *C-O-M-M-I-T-T-E-E.*
- Spell **high.** Get ready. (Signal.) *H-I-G-H.*
- Spell **regard.** Get ready. (Signal.) *R-E-G-A-R-D.*
- Spell **honesty.** Get ready. (Signal.) *H-O-N-E-S-T-Y.*
- Spell **courage.** Get ready. (Signal.) *C-O-U-R-A-G-E.*

Word Building

a. (Write on the board:)

> **1. rhythm + ic =** _____
>
> **2. base + ic =** _____
>
> **3. in + vent + ion + s =** _____
>
> **4. nerve + ous + ness =** _____
>
> **5. con + duce + ive =** _____
>
> **6. pro + vise + ion =** _____

b. You're going to write the words that go in the blanks.

• Number your paper from 1 to 6. ✔

c. Word 1. Write **rhythmic** on your paper. ✔

d. Do the rest of the words on your own. ✔

e. Check your work. Make an **X** next to any word you got wrong.

f. Word 1. Spell **rhythmic.** Get ready. (Tap for each letter.) *R-H-Y-T-H-M-I-C.*

• (Repeat for: **2. basic, 3. inventions, 4. nervousness, 5. conducive, 6. provision.**)

EXERCISE 1

Nonword Base

a. (Write on the board:)

> **duct**

- One morphograph that combines with other morphographs is **duct.**
- What morphograph? (Signal.) *Duct.*
- Spell **duct.** Get ready. (Signal.) *D-U-C-T.*

b. Get ready to spell words that have the morphograph **duct.**

c. First word: **reduction.**
- What's the first morphograph in **reduction?** (Signal.) *Re.*
- Next morphograph? (Signal.) *Duct.*
- Next morphograph? (Signal.) *Ion.*
- Spell **reduction.** Get ready. (Signal.) *R-E-D-U-C-T-I-O-N.*

d. Next word: **conducted.**
- What's the first morphograph in **conducted?** (Signal.) *Con.*
- Next morphograph? (Signal.) *Duct.*
- Next morphograph? (Signal.) *Ed.*
- Spell **conducted.** Get ready. (Signal.) *C-O-N-D-U-C-T-E-D.*

e. (For **product,** have students identify each morphograph and spell the entire word.)

EXERCISE 2

Sentence

a. (Write on the board:)

> **The committee had high regard for honesty and courage.**

- I'll read the sentence on the board: **The committee had high regard for honesty and courage.**
- Let's spell some of those words.

b. Spell **committee.** Get ready. (Signal.) *C-O-M-M-I-T-T-E-E.*
- Spell **high.** Get ready. (Signal.) *H-I-G-H.*
- Spell **regard.** Get ready. (Signal.) *R-E-G-A-R-D.*
- Spell **honesty.** Get ready. (Signal.) *H-O-N-E-S-T-Y.*
- Spell **courage.** Get ready. (Signal.) *C-O-U-R-A-G-E.*

c. (Erase the board.)

d. Now let's spell some of the words in that sentence without looking.
- Spell **committee.** Get ready. (Signal.) *C-O-M-M-I-T-T-E-E.*
- Spell **high.** Get ready. (Signal.) *H-I-G-H.*
- Spell **regard.** Get ready. (Signal.) *R-E-G-A-R-D.*
- Spell **honesty.** Get ready. (Signal.) *H-O-N-E-S-T-Y.*
- Spell **courage.** Get ready. (Signal.) *C-O-U-R-A-G-E.*

EXERCISE 3

Spelling Review

a. Get ready to spell and write some words.

b. Word 1 is **union.**
- What word? (Signal.) *Union.*
- Spell **union.** Get ready. (Signal.) *U-N-I-O-N.*
- Write it. ✔

c. Word 2 is **protection.**
- What word? (Signal.) *Protection.*
- Spell **protection.** Get ready. (Signal.) *P-R-O-T-E-C-T-I-O-N.*
- Write it. ✔

d. (Repeat step c for: **3. scrubbed, 4. people, 5. valuable, 6. resolving.**)

e. I'll spell each word.
- Put an **X** next to any word you missed and write that word correctly.
- (Spell each word twice. Write the words on the board as you spell them.)

Word Introduction

a. (Write on the board:)

> today
> yesterday
> tomorrow
> afternoon
> evening
> morning

b. Get ready to read these words.
- First word: **today.** What word? (Signal.) *Today.*
c. Next word: **yesterday.** What word? (Signal.) *Yesterday.*
- (Repeat for: **tomorrow, afternoon, evening, morning.**)
d. Now spell those words.
- Spell **today.** Get ready. (Signal.) *T-O-D-A-Y.*
e. Spell **yesterday.** Get ready. (Signal.) *Y-E-S-T-E-R-D-A-Y.*
- (Repeat for: **tomorrow, afternoon, evening, morning.**)
f. (Erase the board.)
- Spell the words without looking.
g. Spell **today.** Get ready. (Signal.) *T-O-D-A-Y.*
h. Spell **yesterday.** Get ready. (Signal.) *Y-E-S-T-E-R-D-A-Y.*
- (Repeat for: **tomorrow, afternoon, evening, morning.**)
i. Get ready to write those words.
j. First word: **today.** Write it. ✔
- (Repeat for: **yesterday, tomorrow, afternoon, evening, morning.**)

Sentence

a. You're going to write this sentence: **The committee had high regard for honesty and courage.**
b. Say the sentence. Get ready. (Signal.) *The committee had high regard for honesty and courage.*
c. Write the sentence. ✔

d. (Write on the board:)

> **The committee had high regard for honesty and courage.**

e. Check your work. Make an **X** next to any word you got wrong. ✔

Prompted Review

a. (Write on the board:)

> 1. rhythmic
> 2. childishly
> 3. briefly
> 4. vision
> 5. inspection
> 6. carriage

b. Word 1 is **rhythmic.** Spell **rhythmic.** Get ready. (Signal.) *R-H-Y-T-H-M-I-C.*
c. Word 2 is **childishly.** Spell **childishly.** Get ready. (Signal.) *C-H-I-L-D-I-S-H-L-Y.*
d. (Repeat step c for: **3. briefly, 4. vision, 5. inspection, 6. carriage.**)
e. (Erase the board.)
- Now spell those words without looking.
f. Word 1 is **rhythmic.** Spell **rhythmic.** Get ready. (Signal.) *R-H-Y-T-H-M-I-C.*
g. Word 2 is **childishly.** Spell **childishly.** Get ready. (Signal.) *C-H-I-L-D-I-S-H-L-Y.*
h. (Repeat step g for: **3. briefly, 4. vision, 5. inspection, 6. carriage.**)
i. (Give individual turns on: **1. rhythmic, 2. childishly, 3. briefly, 4. vision, 5. inspection, 6. carriage.**)

EXERCISE 1

Affix Introduction

a. (Write on the board:)

> 1. trans + form =
> 2. trans + action =
> 3. trans + port =

- All these words have the morphograph **trans.**
b. Number your paper from 1 to 3. ✔
c. Add the morphographs together to make new words. Write just the new words. ✔
d. Check your work. Make an **X** next to any word you got wrong.
e. Word 1. Spell **transform.** Get ready. (Tap for each letter.) *T-R-A-N-S-F-O-R-M.*
- (Repeat for: **2. transaction, 3. transport.**)

EXERCISE 2

Word Building

a. (Write on the board:)

> 1. style + ish + ly = _____
> 2. pro + duct + ive = _____
> 3. muse + ic = _____
> 4. dis + ease + ed = _____
> 5. fury + ous + ly = _____
> 6. re + tract + ion = _____

b. You're going to write the words that go in the blanks.
- Number your paper from 1 to 6. ✔
c. Word 1. Write **stylishly** on your paper. ✔
d. Do the rest of the words on your own. ✔
e. Check your work. Make an **X** next to any word you got wrong.
f. Word 1. Spell **stylishly.** Get ready. (Tap for each letter.) *S-T-Y-L-I-S-H-L-Y.*
- (Repeat for: **2. productive, 3. music, 4. diseased, 5. furiously, 6. retraction.**)

EXERCISE 3

Spelling Review

a. Get ready to spell words.
b. Word 1 is **unhealthy.**
- What word? (Signal.) *Unhealthy.*
- Spell **unhealthy.** Get ready. (Signal.) *U-N-H-E-A-L-T-H-Y.*
c. Word 2 is **physical.**
- What word? (Signal.) *Physical.*
- Spell **physical.** Get ready. (Signal.) *P-H-Y-S-I-C-A-L.*
d. (Repeat step c for: **3. childishness, 4. productive, 5. diseased, 6. today.**)
e. (Give individual turns on: **1. unhealthy, 2. physical, 3. childishness, 4. productive, 5. diseased, 6. today.**)

EXERCISE 1

Nonword Base

a. (Write on the board:)

> **fer**

- One morphograph that cannot stand alone is **fer.**
- What morphograph? (Signal.) *Fer.*
- Spell **fer.** Get ready. (Signal.) *F-E-R.*

b. Get ready to spell words that have the morphograph **fer.**

c. First word: **refer.**
- What's the first morphograph in **refer?** (Signal.) *Re.*
- Next morphograph? (Signal.) *Fer.*
- Spell **refer.** Get ready. (Signal.) *R-E-F-E-R.*

d. Next word: **transfer.**
- What's the first morphograph in **transfer?** (Signal.) *Trans.*
- Next morphograph? (Signal.) *Fer.*
- Spell **transfer.** Get ready. (Signal.) *T-R-A-N-S-F-E-R.*

e. (For **confer** and **defer,** have students identify each morphograph and spell each entire word.)

EXERCISE 2

Morphographic Analysis

a. (Write on the board:)

> 1. reduction =
> 2. babies =
> 3. expression =
> 4. transported =
> 5. stepping =
> 6. basic =

- Copy the board. ✔
- Write the morphographs in each word after the equal sign. Put plus signs between the morphographs. ✔

b. (Change the board to show:)

> 1. **reduction** = re + duct + ion
> 2. **babies** = baby + es
> 3. **expression** = ex + press + ion
> 4. **transported** = trans + port + ed
> 5. **stepping** = step + ing
> 6. **basic** = base + ic

c. Check your work. Make an **X** next to any word you got wrong.

EXERCISE 3

Prompted Review

a. (Write on the board:)

> 1. tomorrow
> 2. science
> 3. reaction
> 4. rhythm
> 5. inspection
> 6. grief

b. Word 1 is **tomorrow.** Spell **tomorrow.** Get ready. (Signal.) *T-O-M-O-R-R-O-W.*

c. Word 2 is **science.** Spell **science.** Get ready. (Signal.) *S-C-I-E-N-C-E.*

d. (Repeat step c for: **3. reaction, 4. rhythm, 5. inspection, 6. grief.**)

e. (Erase the board.)
- Now spell those words without looking.

f. Word 1 is **tomorrow.** Spell **tomorrow.** Get ready. (Signal.) *T-O-M-O-R-R-O-W.*

g. Word 2 is **science.** Spell **science.** Get ready. (Signal.) *S-C-I-E-N-C-E.*

h. (Repeat step g for: **3. reaction, 4. rhythm, 5. inspection, 6. grief.**)

i. (Give individual turns on: **1. tomorrow, 2. science, 3. reaction, 4. rhythm, 5. inspection, 6. grief.**)

EXERCISE 1

Word Introduction

a. (Write on the board:)

> tragic
> comic
> critic
> medic
> pulse
> magic

b. Get ready to read these words.
- First word: **tragic.** What word? (Signal.) *Tragic.*
c. Next word: **comic.** What word? (Signal.) *Comic.*
- (Repeat for: **critic, medic, pulse, magic.**)
d. Now spell those words.
- Spell **tragic.** Get ready. (Signal.) *T-R-A-G-I-C.*
e. Spell **comic.** Get ready. (Signal.) *C-O-M-I-C.*
- (Repeat for: **critic, medic, pulse, magic.**)
f. (Erase the board.)
- Spell the words without looking.
g. Spell **tragic.** Get ready. (Signal.) *T-R-A-G-I-C.*
h. Spell **comic.** Get ready. (Signal.) *C-O-M-I-C.*
- (Repeat for: **critic, medic, pulse, magic.**)
i. Get ready to write those words.
j. First word: **tragic.** Write it. ✔
- (Repeat for: **comic, critic, medic, pulse, magic.**)

EXERCISE 2

Word Building

a. (Write on the board:)

> 1. de + fer + ment = _____
> 2. pro + duct + ion = _____
> 3. style + ish + ly = _____
> 4. rhythm + s = _____
> 5. pro + tect + ive = _____
> 6. re + act + ive +ly = _____

b. You're going to write the words that go in the blanks.
- Number your paper from 1 to 6. ✔
c. Word 1. Write **deferment** on your paper. ✔
d. Do the rest of the words on your own. ✔
e. Check your work. Make an **X** next to any word you got wrong.
f. Word 1. Spell **deferment.** Get ready. (Tap for each letter.) *D-E-F-E-R-M-E-N-T.*
- (Repeat for: **2. production, 3. stylishly, 4. rhythms, 5. protective, 6. reactively.**)

EXERCISE 3

Spelling Review

a. Get ready to spell some words.
b. Word 1 is **thoughtlessly.**
- What word? (Signal.) *Thoughtlessly.*
- Spell **thoughtlessly.** Get ready. (Signal.) *T-H-O-U-G-H-T-L-E-S-S-L-Y.*
c. Word 2 is **stretcher.**
- What word? (Signal.) *Stretcher.*
- Spell **stretcher.** Get ready. (Signal.) *S-T-R-E-T-C-H-E-R.*
d. (Repeat step c for: **3. photographing, 4. retained, 5. reception, 6. music.**)
e. (Give individual turns on: **1. thoughtlessly, 2. stretcher, 3. photographing, 4. retained, 5. reception, 6. music.**)

EXERCISE 1

Affix Introduction

a. (Write on the board:)

> 1. ap + point =
> 2. ap + prove =
> 3. ap + praise =

- All these words have the morphograph **ap.**
b. Number your paper from 1 to 3. ✔
c. Add the morphographs together to make new words. Write just the new words. ✔
d. Check your work. Make an **X** next to any word you got wrong.
e. Word 1. Spell **appoint.** Get ready. (Tap for each letter.) *A-P-P-O-I-N-T.*
- (Repeat for: **2. approve, 3. appraise.**)

EXERCISE 2

Word Building

a. (Write on the board:)

> 1. govern + ment + al = _____
> 2. ex + pel = _____
> 3. in + act + ive = _____
> 4. con + form + ing = _____
> 5. con + cept + ion = _____
> 6. mis + in + form + ed = _____

b. You're going to write the words that go in the blanks.
- Number your paper from 1 to 6. ✔
c. Word 1. Write **governmental** on your paper. ✔
d. Do the rest of the words on your own. ✔
e. Check your work. Make an **X** next to any word you got wrong.
f. Word 1. Spell **governmental.** Get ready. (Tap for each letter.) *G-O-V-E-R-N-M-E-N-T-A-L.*
- (Repeat for: **2. expel, 3. inactive, 4. conforming, 5. conception, 6. misinformed.**)

EXERCISE 3

Prompted Review

a. (Write on the board:)

> 1. magic
> 2. transfer
> 3. yesterday
> 4. thirstiest
> 5. committee
> 6. dishonestly

b. Word 1 is **magic.** Spell **magic.** Get ready. (Signal.) *M-A-G-I-C.*
c. Word 2 is **transfer.** Spell **transfer.** Get ready. (Signal.) *T-R-A-N-S-F-E-R.*
d. (Repeat step c for: **3. yesterday, 4. thirstiest, 5. committee, 6. dishonestly.**)
e. (Erase the board.)
- Now spell those words without looking.
f. Word 1 is **magic.** Spell **magic.** Get ready. (Signal.) *M-A-G-I-C.*
g. Word 2 is **transfer.** Spell **transfer.** Get ready. (Signal.) *T-R-A-N-S-F-E-R.*
h. (Repeat step g for: **3. yesterday, 4. thirstiest, 5. committee, 6. dishonestly.**)
i. (Give individual turns on: **1. magic, 2. transfer, 3. yesterday, 4. thirstiest, 5. committee, 6. dishonestly.**)

EXERCISE 1

Word Introduction

a. (Write on the board:)

> show
> blow
> know
> grow
> throw
> draw

b. Get ready to read these words.
- First word: **show.** What word? (Signal.) *Show.*

c. Next word: **blow.** What word? (Signal.) *Blow.*
- (Repeat for: **know, grow, throw, draw.**)

d. Now spell those words.
- Spell **show.** Get ready. (Signal.) *S-H-O-W.*

e. Spell **blow.** Get ready. (Signal.) *B-L-O-W.*
- (Repeat for: **know, grow, throw, draw.**)

f. (Erase the board.)
- Spell the words without looking.

g. Spell **show.** Get ready. (Signal.) *S-H-O-W.*

h. Spell **blow.** Get ready. (Signal.) *B-L-O-W.*
- (Repeat for: **know, grow, throw, draw.**)

i. Get ready to write those words.

j. First word: **show.** Write it.
- (Repeat for: **blow, know, grow, throw, draw.**)

EXERCISE 2

Morphographic Analysis

a. (Write on the board:)

> 1. appointment =
> 2. informally =
> 3. repulsive =
> 4. rediscovered =
> 5. respectable =
> 6. beautifully =

- Copy the board. ✔
- Write the morphographs in each word after the equal sign. Put plus signs between the morphographs. ✔

b. (Change the board to show:)

> 1. **appointment** = ap + point + ment
> 2. **informally** = in + form + al + ly
> 3. **repulsive** = re + pulse + ive
> 4. **rediscovered** =
>   re + dis + cover + ed
> 5. **respectable** = re + spect + able
> 6. **beautifully** = beauty + ful + ly

c. Check your work. Make an **X** next to any word you got wrong.

EXERCISE 3

Prompted Review

a. (Write on the board:)

> 1. tragic
> 2. appraisal
> 3. infer
> 4. transported
> 5. committee
> 6. briefest

b. Word 1 is **tragic.** Spell **tragic.** Get ready. (Signal.) *T-R-A-G-I-C.*

c. Word 2 is **appraisal.** Spell **appraisal.** Get ready. (Signal.) *A-P-P-R-A-I-S-A-L.*

d. (Repeat step c for: **3. infer, 4. transported, 5. committee, 6. briefest.**)

e. (Erase the board.)
- Now spell those words without looking.

f. Word 1 is **tragic.** Spell **tragic.** Get ready. (Signal.) *T-R-A-G-I-C.*

g. Word 2 is **appraisal.** Spell **appraisal.** Get ready. (Signal.) *A-P-P-R-A-I-S-A-L.*

h. (Repeat step g for: **3. infer, 4. transported, 5. committee, 6. briefest.**)

i. (Give individual turns on: **1. tragic, 2. appraisal, 3. infer, 4. transported, 5. committee, 6. briefest.**)

EXERCISE 1

Test

a. Today you have a spelling test. Number your lined paper from 1 through 10. ✔

b. Word 1 is **governmental.** What word? (Signal.) *Governmental.*

• Write the word **governmental.** ✔

c. Word 2 is **stylishly.** What word? (Signal.) *Stylishly.*

• Write the word **stylishly.** ✔

d. Word 3 is **committee.** What word? (Signal.) *Committee.*

• Write the word **committee.** ✔

e. Word 4 is **expression.** What word? (Signal.) *Expression.*

• Write the word **expression.** ✔

f. Word 5 is **critic.** What word? (Signal.) *Critic.*

• Write the word **critic.** ✔

g. Word 6 is **yesterday.** What word? (Signal.) *Yesterday.*

• Write the word **yesterday.** ✔

h. Word 7 is **development.** What word? (Signal.) *Development.*

• Write the word **development.** ✔

i. Word 8 is **famously.** What word? (Signal.) *Famously.*

• Write the word **famously.** ✔

j. Word 9 is **speediest.** What word? (Signal.) *Speediest.*

• Write the word **speediest.** ✔

k. Word 10 is **signal.** What word? (Signal.) *Signal.*

• Write the word **signal.** ✔

l. Pick up your red pen. ✔
   Make an **X** next to any word you spelled wrong.

• (Write on the board:)

1. governmental	6. yesterday
2. stylishly	7. development
3. committee	8. famously
4. expression	9. speediest
5. critic	10. signal

• Write the correct spelling next to any word you spelled wrong.
   (Observe students and give feedback.)

EXERCISE 1
Word Introduction

a. (Write on the board:)

> **sphere**
> **cycle**

b. Get ready to read these words.
- First word: **sphere.** What word? (Signal.) *Sphere.*
c. Next word: **cycle.** What word? (Signal.) *Cycle.*
d. Now spell those words.
- Spell **sphere.** Get ready. (Signal.) *S-P-H-E-R-E.*
e. Spell **cycle.** Get ready. (Signal.) *C-Y-C-L-E.*
f. (Erase the board.)
- Spell the words without looking.
g. Spell **sphere.** Get ready. (Signal.) *S-P-H-E-R-E.*
h. Spell **cycle.** Get ready. (Signal.) *C-Y-C-L-E.*
i. Get ready to write those words.
j. First word: **sphere.** Write it. ✔
- (Repeat for: **cycle.**)

EXERCISE 2
Word Building

a. (Write on the board:)

> **1. ap + praise + al = _____**
> **2. show + ing = _____**
> **3. medic + al = _____**
> **4. trans + form + ed = _____**
> **5. pity + ful + ly = _____**
> **6. re + vise + ion = _____**

b. You're going to write the words that go in the blanks.
- Number your paper from 1 to 6. ✔
c. Word 1. Write **appraisal** on your paper. ✔
d. Do the rest of the words on your own. ✔
e. Check your work. Make an **X** next to any word you got wrong.
f. Word 1. Spell **appraisal.** Get ready. (Tap for each letter.) *A-P-P-R-A-I-S-A-L.*
- (Repeat for: **2. showing, 3. medical, 4. transformed, 5. pitifully, 6. revision.**)

EXERCISE 3
Spelling Review

a. Get ready to spell words.
b. Word 1 is **unplanned.**
- What word? (Signal.) *Unplanned.*
- Spell **unplanned.** Get ready. (Signal.) *U-N-P-L-A-N-N-E-D.*
c. Word 2 is **courage.**
- What word? (Signal.) *Courage.*
- Spell **courage.** Get ready. (Signal.) *C-O-U-R-A-G-E.*
d. (Repeat step c for: **3. repel, 4. development, 5. dangerous, 6. preserve, 7. signal, 8. yesterday.**)
e (Give individual turns on: **1. unplanned, 2. courage, 3. repel, 4. development, 5. dangerous, 6. preserve, 7. signal, 8. yesterday.**)

EXERCISE 1

Nonword Base

a. (Write on the board:)

> **tent**

- One morphograph that combines with other morphographs is **tent**.
- What morphograph? (Signal.) *Tent.*
- Spell **tent**. Get ready. (Signal.) *T-E-N-T.*

b. Get ready to spell words that have the morphograph **tent**.

c. First word: **content**.
- What's the first morphograph in **content**? (Signal.) *Con.*
- Next morphograph? (Signal.) *Tent.*
- Spell **content**. Get ready. (Signal.) *C-O-N-T-E-N-T.*

d. Next word: **intention**.
- What's the first morphograph in **intention**? (Signal.) *In.*
- Next morphograph? (Signal.) *Tent.*
- Next morphograph? (Signal.) *Ion.*
- Spell **intention**. Get ready. (Signal.) *I-N-T-E-N-T-I-O-N.*

e. (For **extent** and **retention**, have students identify each morphograph and spell each entire word.)

EXERCISE 2

Morphographic Analysis

a. (Write on the board:)

> 1. approval =
> 2. deferment =
> 3. readiness =
> 4. prospective =
> 5. structural =
> 6. scariest =

- Copy the board. ✔
- Write the morphographs in each word after the equal sign. Put plus signs between the morphographs. ✔

b. (Change the board to show:)

> 1. **approval** = ap + prove + al
> 2. **deferment** = de + fer + ment
> 3. **readiness** = read + y + ness
> 4. **prospective** = pro + spect + ive
> 5. **structural** = struct + ure + al
> 6. **scariest** = scare + y + est

c. Check your work. Make an **X** next to any word you got wrong.

EXERCISE 3

Prompted Review

a. (Write on the board:)

> 1. regardless
> 2. committee
> 3. drawing
> 4. courage
> 5. rhythmic
> 6. diseased

b. Word 1 is **regardless**. Spell **regardless**. Get ready. (Signal.) *R-E-G-A-R-D-L-E-S-S.*

c. Word 2 is **committee**. Spell **committee**. Get ready. (Signal.) *C-O-M-M-I-T-T-E-E.*

d. (Repeat step c for: **3. drawing, 4. courage, 5. rhythmic, 6. diseased.**)

e. (Erase the board.)
- Now spell those words without looking.

f. Word 1 is **regardless**. Spell **regardless**. Get ready. (Signal.) *R-E-G-A-R-D-L-E-S-S.*

g. Word 2 is **committee**. Spell **committee**. Get ready. (Signal.) *C-O-M-M-I-T-T-E-E.*

h. (Repeat step g for: **3. drawing, 4. courage, 5. rhythmic, 6. diseased.**)

i. (Give individual turns on: **1. regardless, 2. committee, 3. drawing, 4. courage, 5. rhythmic, 6. diseased.**)

EXERCISE 1

EN Variation

a. (Write on the board:)

> **1. show + en = shown**

b. Here is a new rule: When a word ends with the letter **w** and you add **e-n,** drop the **e.**

c. (Point to **show.**)

- The word **show** ends with the letter **w.** So we drop the **e** from **e-n** when we write **shown.**

- (Cross out the **e** in **en.**)

> **1. show + e̶ = shown**

d. The word **draw** ends with the letter **w.** So tell me how to spell the word **drawn.** (Pause.) Get ready. (Signal.) *D-R-A-W-N.*

e. What letter does the word **grow** end with? (Signal.) *W.*

f. So tell me how to spell the word **grown.** (Pause.) Get ready. (Signal.) *G-R-O-W-N.*

g. What letter does the word **throw** end with? (Signal.) *W.*

h. So tell me how to spell the word **thrown.** (Pause.) Get ready. (Signal.) *T-H-R-O-W-N.*

i. (Change the board to show:)

> **1. show + e̶n = shown**
> **2. sew + en =**
> **3. ripe + en =**
> **4. grow + en =**
> **5. prove + en =**
> **6. blow + en =**

j. Copy words 2 through 6 on your paper. Then add the morphographs together. Some of the words end with **w.** Some don't. ✔

k. I'll spell each word.

- Put an **X** next to any word you missed and write that word correctly.

- (Spell each word twice. Write the words on the board as you spell them.)

> **2. sew + en = sewn**
> **3. ripe + en = ripen**
> **4. grow + en = grown**
> **5. prove + en = proven**
> **6. blow + en = blown**

EXERCISE 2

Word Building

a. (Write on the board:)

> **1. please + ure = _____**
> **2. con + tent + ment = _____**
> **3. cycle + ic = _____**
> **4. trans + late + ion = _____**
> **5. pre + script + ion = _____**
> **6. in + tent + ion = _____**

b. You're going to write the words that go in the blanks.

- Number your paper from 1 to 6. ✔

c. Word 1. Write **pleasure** on your paper. ✔

d. Do the rest of the words on your own. ✔

e. Check your work. Make an **X** next to any word you got wrong.

f. Word 1. Spell **pleasure.** Get ready. (Tap for each letter.) *P-L-E-A-S-U-R-E.*

- (Repeat for: **2. contentment, 3. cyclic, 4. translation, 5. prescription, 6. intention.**)

EXERCISE 3

Spelling Review

a. Get ready to spell words.

b. Word 1 is **produce.**

- What word? (Signal.) *Produce.*

- Spell **produce.** Get ready. (Signal.) *P-R-O-D-U-C-E.*

c. Word 2 is **receptive.**

- What word? (Signal.) *Receptive.*

- Spell **receptive.** Get ready. (Signal.) *R-E-C-E-P-T-I-V-E.*

d. (Repeat step c for: **3. inaction, 4. nervously, 5. studies, 6. describing.**)

e. (Give individual turns on: **1. produce, 2. receptive, 3. inaction, 4. nervously, 5. studies, 6. describing.**)

EXERCISE 1

EN Variation

a. (Write on the board:)

> **1. draw + en = drawn**

b. Remember, when a word ends with the letter **w** and you add **e-n,** drop the **e.**

c. (Point to **draw.**)

• The word **draw** ends with the letter **w.** So we drop the **e** from **e-n** when we write **drawn.**

• (Cross out the **e** in **en.**)

> **1. draw + én = drawn**

d. What letter does the word **grow** end with? (Signal.) *W.*

e. So tell me how to spell the word **grown.** (Pause.) Get ready. (Signal.) *G-R-O-W-N.*

f. (Change the board to show:)

> **1. draw + én = drawn**
> **2. know + en =**
> **3. take + en =**
> **4. blow + en =**
> **5. show + en =**
> **6. mad + en =**

g. Copy words 2 through 6 on your paper. Then add the morphographs together. Some of the words end in **w.** Some don't. (Observe students and give feedback.)

h. I'll spell each word.

• Put an **X** next to any word you missed and write that word correctly.

• (Spell each word twice. Write the words on the board as you spell them.)

> **2. know + en = known**
> **3. take + en = taken**
> **4. blow + en = blown**
> **5. show + en = shown**
> **6. mad + en = madden**

EXERCISE 2

Sentence Variation

a. Get ready to write on lined paper.

• You are going to write a sentence made up of words you know how to spell. Put the right punctuation mark at the end of the sentence.

b. The sentence is **The science committee studied a photograph yesterday afternoon.**

• Say that sentence. Get ready. (Signal.) *The science committee studied a photograph yesterday afternoon.*

• (Repeat until firm.)

c. Write it. ✔

d. Get ready to check your spelling. Put an **X** next to any word you missed.

e. Spell **science.** Get ready. (Signal.) *S-C-I-E-N-C-E.*

• Check it. ✔

f. Spell **committee.** Get ready. (Signal.) *C-O-M-M-I-T-T-E-E.*

• Check it. ✔

• (Repeat for: **studied, photograph, yesterday, afternoon.**)

g. What punctuation mark did you put at the end of the sentence? (Signal.) *A period.*

• Check it. ✔

h. Fix any words you missed.

EXERCISE 3

Spelling Review

a. Get ready to spell words.

b. Word 1 is **scrubbing.**

• What word? (Signal.) *Scrubbing.*

• Spell **scrubbing.** Get ready. (Signal.) *S-C-R-U-B-B-I-N-G.*

c. Word 2 is **sluggishness.**

• What word? (Signal.) *Sluggishness.*

• Spell **sluggishness.** Get ready. (Signal.) *S-L-U-G-G-I-S-H-N-E-S-S.*

d. (Repeat step c for: **3. misshapen, 4. prediction, 5. sphere, 6. fanciest.**)

e. (Give individual turns on: **1. scrubbing, 2. sluggishness, 3. misshapen, 4. prediction, 5. sphere, 6. fanciest.**)

EXERCISE 1

Word Introduction

a. (Write on the board:)

> merge
> ground
> sleep
> shame
> while

b. Get ready to read these words.
- First word: **merge.** What word? (Signal.) *Merge.*
c. Next word: **ground.** What word? (Signal.) *Ground.*
- (Repeat for: **sleep, shame, while.**)
d. Now spell those words.
- Spell **merge.** Get ready. (Signal.) *M-E-R-G-E.*
e. Spell **ground.** Get ready. (Signal.) *G-R-O-U-N-D.*
- (Repeat for: **sleep, shame, while.**)
f. (Erase the board.)
- Spell the words without looking.
g. Spell **merge.** Get ready. (Signal.) *M-E-R-G-E.*
h. Spell **ground.** Get ready. (Signal.) *G-R-O-U-N-D.*
- (Repeat for: **sleep, shame, while.**)
i. Get ready to write those words.
j. First word: **merge.** Write it.
- (Repeat for: **ground, sleep, shame, while.**)

EXERCISE 2

Morphographic Analysis

a. (Write on the board:)

> 1. disgraceful =
> 2. attractive =
> 3. reduction =
> 4. resigned =
> 5. dishonest =

- Copy the board. ✔
- Write the morphographs in each word after the equal sign. Put plus signs between the morphographs. ✔

b. (Change the board to show:)

> 1. disgraceful = dis + grace + ful
> 2. attractive = attract + ive
> 3. reduction = re + duct + ion
> 4. resigned = re + sign + ed
> 5. dishonest = dis + honest

c. Check your work. Make an **X** next to any word you got wrong.

EXERCISE 3

Prompted Review

a. (Write on the board:)

> 1. encouragement
> 2. provisional
> 3. disappointment
> 4. misconception
> 5. expressively
> 6. resigned

b. Word 1 is **encouragement.** Spell **encouragement.** Get ready. (Signal.) *E-N-C-O-U-R-A-G-E-M-E-N-T.*
c. Word 2 is **provisional.** Spell **provisional.** Get ready. (Signal.) *P-R-O-V-I-S-I-O-N-A-L.*
d. (Repeat step c for: **3. disappointment, 4. misconception, 5. expressively, 6. resigned.**)
e. (Erase the board.)
- Now spell those words without looking.
f. Word 1 is **encouragement.** Spell **encouragement.** Get ready. (Signal.) *E-N-C-O-U-R-A-G-E-M-E-N-T.*
g. Word 2 is **provisional.** Spell **provisional.** Get ready. (Signal.) *P-R-O-V-I-S-I-O-N-A-L.*
h. (Repeat step g for: **3. disappointment, 4. misconception, 5. expressively, 6. resigned.**)
i. (Give individual turns on: **1. encouragement, 2. provisional, 3. disappointment, 4. misconception, 5. expressively, 6. resigned.**)

LESSON 66

EXERCISE 1

Sentence

a. (Write on the board:)

> **Two scientists and their assistants were in an automobile accident.**

- I'll read the sentence on the board. **Two scientists and their assistants were in an automobile accident.**
- Let's spell some of those words.
b. Spell **Two.** Get ready. (Signal.) *T-W-O.*
- Spell **scientists.** Get ready. (Signal.) *S-C-I-E-N-T-I-S-T-S.*
- Spell **their.** Get ready. (Signal.) *T-H-E-I-R.*
- Spell **assistants.** Get ready. (Signal.) *A-S-S-I-S-T-A-N-T-S.*
- Spell **were.** Get ready. (Signal.) *W-E-R-E.*
- Spell **automobile.** Get ready. (Signal.) *A-U-T-O-M-O-B-I-L-E.*
- Spell **accident.** Get ready. (Signal.) *A-C-C-I-D-E-N-T.*
c. Copy this sentence on lined paper.
d. (Pause, then check and correct.)
- Read the sentence you just copied. Get ready. (Signal.) *Two scientists and their assistants were in an automobile accident.*

EXERCISE 2

Word Building

a. (Write on the board:)

> 1. **sphere + ic + al = _____**
> 2. **re + late + ive = _____**
> 3. **ap + proach = _____**
> 4. **dis + ap + point + ment = _____**
> 5. **sleep + less + ness = _____**
> 6. **ex + tent + ion = _____**

b. You're going to write the words that go in the blanks.
- Number your paper from 1 to 6. ✔
c. Word 1. Write **spherical** on your paper. ✔
d. Do the rest of the words on your own. ✔
e. Check your work. Make an **X** next to any word you got wrong.

f. Word 1. Spell **spherical.** Get ready. (Tap for each letter.) *S-P-H-E-R-I-C-A-L.*
- (Repeat for: **2. relative, 3. approach, 4. disappointment, 5. sleeplessness, 6. extension.**)

EXERCISE 3

Spelling Review

a. Get ready to spell words.
b. Word 1 is **sleepy.**
- What word? (Signal.) *Sleepy.*
- Spell **sleepy.** Get Ready. (Signal.) *S-L-E-E-P-Y.*
c. Word 2 is **rhythm.**
- What word? (Signal.) *Rhythm.*
- Spell **rhythm.** Get Ready. (Signal.) *R-H-Y-T-H-M.*
d. (Repeat step c for: **3. governmental, 4. prescription, 5. transgression, 6. cities.**)
e. (Give individual turns on: **1. sleepy, 2. rhythm, 3. governmental, 4. prescription, 5. transgression, 6. cities.**)

LESSON 67

EXERCISE 1

Sentence

a. (Write on the board:)

> **Two scientists and their assistants were in an automobile accident.**

- I'll read the sentence on the board. **Two scientists and their assistants were in an automobile accident.**
- Let's spell some of those words.

b. Spell **Two.** Get ready. (Signal.) *T-W-O.*
- Spell **scientists.** Get ready. (Signal.) *S-C-I-E-N-T-I-S-T-S.*
- Spell **their.** Get ready. (Signal.) *T-H-E-I-R.*
- Spell **assistants.** Get ready. (Signal.) *A-S-S-I-S-T-A-N-T-S.*
- Spell **were.** Get ready. (Signal.) *W-E-R-E.*
- Spell **automobile.** Get ready. (Signal.) *A-U-T-O-M-O-B-I-L-E.*
- Spell **accident.** Get ready. (Signal.) *A-C-C-I-D-E-N-T.*

c. (Erase the board.)

d. Now let's spell some of the words in that sentence without looking.
- Spell **Two.** Get ready. (Signal.) *T-W-O.*
- Spell **scientists.** Get ready. (Signal.) *S-C-I-E-N-T-I-S-T-S.*
- Spell **their.** Get ready. (Signal.) *T-H-E-I-R.*
- Spell **assistants.** Get ready. (Signal.) *A-S-S-I-S-T-A-N-T-S.*
- Spell **were.** Get ready. (Signal.) *W-E-R-E.*
- Spell **automobile.** Get ready. (Signal.) *A-U-T-O-M-O-B-I-L-E.*
- Spell **accident.** Get ready. (Signal.) *A-C-C-I-D-E-N-T.*

EXERCISE 2

Sentence Variation

a. Get ready to write on lined paper.
- You are going to write a sentence made up of words you know how to spell. Put the right punctuation mark at the end of the sentence.

b. The sentence is **The mother felt powerless when her child went to science class.**
- Say that sentence. Get ready. (Signal.) *The mother felt powerless when her child went to science class.*
- (Repeat until firm.)

c. Write it. ✔

d. Get ready to check your spelling. Put an **X** next to any word you missed.

e. Spell **mother.** Get ready. (Signal.) *M-O-T-H-E-R.*
- Check it. ✔

f. Spell **felt.** Get ready. (Signal.) *F-E-L-T.*
- Check it. ✔
- (Repeat for: **powerless, when, her, child, went, science, class.**)

g. What end mark did you put at the end of the sentence? (Signal.) *A period.*
- Check it. ✔

h. Fix any words you missed.

EXERCISE 3

Prompted Review

a. (Write on the board:)

> 1. approach   4. reception
> 2. merging   5. creatively
> 3. honest   6. cycling

b. Word 1 is **approach.** Spell **approach.** Get ready. (Signal.) *A-P-P-R-O-A-C-H.*

c. Word 2 is **merging.** Spell **merging.** Get ready. (Signal.) *M-E-R-G-I-N-G.*

d. (Repeat step c for: **3. honest, 4. reception, 5. creatively, 6. cycling.**)

e. (Erase the board.)
- Now spell those words without looking.

f. Word 1 is **approach.** Spell **approach.** Get ready. (Signal.) *A-P-P-R-O-A-C-H.*

g. Word 2 is **merging.** Spell **merging.** Get ready. (Signal.) *M-E-R-G-I-N-G.*

h. (Repeat step g for: **3. honest, 4. reception, 5. creatively, 6. cycling.**)

i. (Give individual turns on: **1. approach, 2. merging, 3. honest, 4. reception, 5. creatively, 6. cycling.**)

EXERCISE 1

Sentence

a. (Write on the board:)

> **Two scientists and their assistants were in an automobile accident.**

- I'll read the sentence on the board. **Two scientists and their assistants were in an automobile accident.**
- Let's spell some of those words.

b. Spell **Two.** Get ready. (Signal.) *T-W-O.*
- Spell **scientists.** Get ready. (Signal.) *S-C-I-E-N-T-I-S-T-S.*
- Spell **their.** Get ready. (Signal.) *T-H-E-I-R.*
- Spell **assistants.** Get ready. (Signal.) *A-S-S-I-S-T-A-N-T-S.*
- Spell **were.** Get ready. (Signal.) *W-E-R-E.*
- Spell **automobile.** Get ready. (Signal.) *A-U-T-O-M-O-B-I-L-E.*
- Spell **accident.** Get ready. (Signal.) *A-C-C-I-D-E-N-T.*

c. (Erase the board.)

d. Now let's spell some of the words in that sentence without looking.
- Spell **Two.** Get ready. (Signal.) *T-W-O.*
- Spell **scientists.** Get ready. (Signal.) *S-C-I-E-N-T-I-S-T-S.*
- Spell **their.** Get ready. (Signal.) *T-H-E-I-R.*
- Spell **assistants.** Get ready. (Signal.) *A-S-S-I-S-T-A-N-T-S.*
- Spell **were.** Get ready. (Signal.) *W-E-R-E.*
- Spell **automobile.** Get ready. (Signal.) *A-U-T-O-M-O-B-I-L-E.*
- Spell **accident.** Get ready. (Signal.) *A-C-C-I-D-E-N-T.*

EXERCISE 2

Word Building

a. (Write on the board:)

> 1. show + en = _____
> 2. ex + tent + ion = _____
> 3. muse + ic + al = _____
> 4. scene + ic = _____
> 5. ap + praise + al = _____
> 6. trans + act + ion = _____

b. You're going to write the words that go in the blanks.
- Some of these words follow rules you've learned.
- Number your paper from 1 to 6. ✔

c. Word 1. Write **shown** on your paper. ✔

d. Do the rest of the words on your own. ✔

e. Check your work. Make an **X** next to any word you got wrong.

f. Word 1. Spell **shown.** Get ready. (Tap for each letter.) *S-H-O-W-N.*
- (Repeat for: **2. extension, 3. musical, 4. scenic, 5. appraisal, 6. transaction.**)

EXERCISE 3

Spelling Review

a. Get ready to spell words.

b. Word 1 is **groundless.**
- What word? (Signal.) *Groundless.*
- Spell **groundless.** Get ready. (Signal.) *G-R-O-U-N-D-L-E-S-S.*

c. Word 2 is **shameful.**
- What word? (Signal.) *Shameful.*
- Spell **shameful.** Get ready. (Signal.) *S-H-A-M-E-F-U-L.*

d. (Repeat step c for: **3. bought, 4. tourists, 5. disarmed, 6. crosses.**)

e. (Give individual turns on: **1. groundless, 2. shameful, 3. bought, 4. tourists, 5. disarmed, 6. crosses.**)

EXERCISE 1

Sentence

a. You're going to write this sentence: **Two scientists and their assistants were in an automobile accident.**

b. Say the sentence. Get ready. (Signal.) *Two scientists and their assistants were in an automobile accident.*

c. Write the sentence. ✔

d. (Write on the board:)

> **Two scientists and their assistants were in an automobile accident.**

e. Check your work. Make an **X** next to any word you got wrong. ✔

EXERCISE 2

Morphographic Analysis

a. (Write on the board:)

> 1. bodies =
> 2. cyclic =
> 3. dropper =
> 4. approval =
> 5. instruction =
> 6. unintended =

- Copy the board. ✔
- Write the morphographs in each word after the equal sign. Put plus signs between the morphographs. ✔

b. (Change the board to show:)

> 1. bodies = body + es
> 2. cyclic = cycle + ic
> 3. dropper = drop + er
> 4. approval = ap + prove + al
> 5. instruction = in + struct + ion
> 6. unintended = un + in + tend + ed

c. Check your work. Make an **X** next to any word you got wrong.

EXERCISE 3

Spelling Review

a. Get ready to spell words.

b. Word 1 is **relative.**
- What word? (Signal.) *Relative.*
- Spell **relative.** Get ready. (Signal.) *R-E-L-A-T-I-V-E.*

c. Word 2 is **resigned.**
- What word? (Signal.) *Resigned.*
- Spell **resigned.** Get ready. (Signal.) *R-E-S-I-G-N-E-D.*

d. (Repeat step c for: **3. translation, 4. perspective, 5. stylishly, 6. nervousness.**)

e. (Give individual turns on: **1. relative, 2. resigned, 3. translation, 4. perspective, 5. stylishly, 6. nervousness.**)

LESSON 70

Test

a. Today you have a spelling test. Number your lined paper from 1 through 10. ✔

b. Word 1 is **nervously.** What word? (Signal.) *Nervously.*

• Write the word **nervously.** ✔

c. Word 2 is **shown.** What word? (Signal.) *Shown.*

• Write the word **shown.** ✔

d. Word 3 is **disappointment.** What word? (Signal.) *Disappointment.*

• Write the word **disappointment.** ✔

e. Word 4 is **committee.** What word? (Signal.) *Committee.*

• Write the word **committee.** ✔

f. Word 5 is **stretcher.** What word? (Signal.) *Stretcher.*

• Write the word **stretcher.** ✔

g. Word 6 is **respectable.** What word? (Signal.) *Respectable.*

• Write the word **respectable.** ✔

h. Word 7 is **simply.** What word? (Signal.) *Simply.*

• Write the word **simply.** ✔

i. Word 8 is **science.** What word? (Signal.) *Science.*

• Write the word **science.** ✔

j. Word 9 is **unions.** What word? (Signal.) *Unions.*

• Write the word **unions.** ✔

k. Word 10 is **marriage.** What word? (Signal.) *Marriage.*

• Write the word **marriage.** ✔

l. Pick up your red pen. ✔
   Make an **X** next to any word you spelled wrong.

• (Write on the board:)

1. nervously	6. respectable
2. shown	7. simply
3. disappointment	8. science
4. committee	9. unions
5. stretcher	10. marriage

• Write the correct spelling next to any word you spelled wrong.
   (Observe students and give feedback.)

EXERCISE 1

Nonword Base

a. (Write on the board:)

> **tend**

- One morphograph that combines with other morphographs is **tend.**
- What morphograph? (Signal.) *Tend.*
- Spell **tend.** Get ready. (Signal.) *T-E-N-D.*

b. Get ready to spell words that have the morphograph **tend.**

c. First word: **pretend.**

- What's the first morphograph in **pretend?** (Signal.) *Pre.*
- Next morphograph? (Signal.) *Tend.*
- Spell **pretend.** Get ready. (Signal.) *P-R-E-T-E-N-D.*

d. Next word: **intend.**

- What's the first morphograph in **intend?** (Signal.) *In.*
- Next morphograph? (Signal.) *Tend.*
- Spell **intend.** Get ready. (Signal.) *I-N-T-E-N-D.*

e. (For **contend** and **extend,** have students identify each morphograph and spell each entire word.)

EXERCISE 2

Sentence

a. (Write on the board:)

> **Some explorers discovered treasure on a magic island.**

- I'll read the sentence on the board. **Some explorers discovered treasure on a magic island.**
- Let's spell some of those words.

b. Spell **Some.** Get ready. (Signal.) *S-O-M-E.*

- Spell **explorers.** Get ready. (Signal.) *E-X-P-L-O-R-E-R-S.*
- Spell **discovered.** Get ready. (Signal.) *D-I-S-C-O-V-E-R-E-D.*
- Spell **treasure.** Get ready. (Signal.) *T-R-E-A-S-U-R-E.*
- Spell **magic.** Get ready. (Signal.) *M-A-G-I-C.*
- Spell **island.** Get ready. (Signal.) *I-S-L-A-N-D.*

c. Copy this sentence on lined paper.

d. (Pause, then check and correct.)

- Read the sentence you just copied. Get ready. (Signal.) *Some explorers discovered treasure on a magic island.*

EXERCISE 3

Prompted Review

a. (Write on the board:)

> 1. throwing
> 2. misinformed
> 3. appointment
> 4. transfer
> 5. tomorrow
> 6. transcribe

b. Word 1 is **throwing.** Spell **throwing.** Get ready. (Signal.) *T-H-R-O-W-I-N-G.*

c. Word 2 is **misinformed.** Spell **misinformed.** Get ready. (Signal.) *M-I-S-I-N-F-O-R-M-E-D.*

d. (Repeat step c for: **3. appointment, 4. transfer, 5. tomorrow, 6. transcribe.**)

e. (Erase the board.)

- Now spell those words without looking.

f. Word 1 is **throwing.** Spell **throwing.** Get ready. (Signal.) *T-H-R-O-W-I-N-G.*

g. Word 2 is **misinformed.** Spell **misinformed.** Get ready. (Signal.) *M-I-S-I-N-F-O-R-M-E-D.*

h. (Repeat step g for: **3. appointment, 4. transfer, 5. tomorrow, 6. transcribe.**)

i. (Give individual turns on: **1. throwing, 2. misinformed, 3. appointment, 4. transfer, 5. tomorrow, 6. transcribe.**)

LESSON 72

EXERCISE 1

Affix Introduction

a. (Write on the board:)

> 1. for + bid =
> 2. for + get =
> 3. for + give =

- All these words have the morphograph **for.**
b. Number your paper from 1 to 3. ✔
c. Add the morphographs together to make new words. Write just the new words. ✔
d. Check your work. Make an **X** next to any word you got wrong.
e. Word 1. Spell **forbid.** Get ready. (Tap for each letter.) *F-O-R-B-I-D.*
- (Repeat for: **2. forget, 3. forgive.**)

EXERCISE 2

Sentence

a. (Write on the board:)

> **Some explorers discovered treasure on a magic island.**

- I'll read the sentence on the board. **Some explorers discovered treasure on a magic island.**
- Let's spell some of those words.
b. Spell **Some.** Get ready. (Signal.) *S-O-M-E.*
- Spell **explorers.** Get ready. (Signal.) *E-X-P-L-O-R-E-R-S.*
- Spell **discovered.** Get ready. (Signal.) *D-I-S-C-O-V-E-R-E-D.*
- Spell **treasure.** Get ready. (Signal.) *T-R-E-A-S-U-R-E.*
- Spell **magic.** Get ready. (Signal.) *M-A-G-I-C.*
- Spell **island.** Get ready. (Signal.) *I-S-L-A-N-D.*
c. (Erase the board.)

d. Now let's spell some of the words in that sentence without looking.
- Spell **Some.** Get ready. (Signal.) *S-O-M-E.*
- Spell **explorers.** Get ready. (Signal.) *E-X-P-L-O-R-E-R-S.*
- Spell **discovered.** Get ready. (Signal.) *D-I-S-C-O-V-E-R-E-D.*
- Spell **treasure.** Get ready. (Signal.) *T-R-E-A-S-U-R-E.*
- Spell **magic.** Get ready. (Signal.) *M-A-G-I-C.*
- Spell **island.** Get ready. (Signal.) *I-S-L-A-N-D.*

EXERCISE 3

Spelling Review

a. You're going to write words.
- Number your paper from 1 to 6. ✔
b. Word 1 is **committee.** Write it. ✔
c. Word 2 is **tragic.** Write it. ✔
d. (Repeat Step c for: **3. chiefly, 4. approve, 5. extend, 6. nastiness.**)
e. Check your work. Make an **X** next to any word you got wrong.
f. Word 1. Spell **committee.** Get ready. (Tap for each letter.) *C-O-M-M-I-T-T-E-E.*
- (Repeat for: **2. tragic, 3. chiefly, 4. approve, 5. extend, 6. nastiness.**)

EXERCISE 1

Word Building

a. (Write on the board:)

> 1. merge + ing = _____
> 2. re + tent + ion = _____
> 3. style + ish + ly = _____
> 4. pre + tend + ing = _____
> 5. shame + less + ly = _____
> 6. trans + form + ing = _____

b. You're going to write the words that go in the blanks.
- Number your paper from 1 to 6. ✔
c. Word 1. Write **merging** on your paper. ✔
d. Do the rest of the words on your own. ✔
e. Check your work. Make an **X** next to any word you got wrong.
f. Word 1. Spell **merging.** Get ready. (Tap for each letter.) *M-E-R-G-I-N-G.*
- (Repeat for: **2. retention, 3. stylishly, 4. pretending, 5. shamelessly, 6. transforming.**)

EXERCISE 2

Sentence

a. (Write on the board:)

> **Some explorers discovered treasure on a magic island.**

- I'll read the sentence on the board. **Some explorers discovered treasure on a magic island.**
- Let's spell some of those words.
b. Spell **Some.** Get ready. (Signal.) *S-O-M-E.*
- Spell **explorers.** Get ready. (Signal.) *E-X-P-L-O-R-E-R-S.*
- Spell **discovered.** Get ready. (Signal.) *D-I-S-C-O-V-E-R-E-D.*
- Spell **treasure.** Get ready. (Signal.) *T-R-E-A-S-U-R-E.*
- Spell **magic.** Get ready. (Signal.) *M-A-G-I-C.*
- Spell **island.** Get ready. (Signal.) *I-S-L-A-N-D.*

c. (Erase the board.)
d. Now let's spell some of the words in that sentence without looking.
- Spell **Some.** Get ready. (Signal.) *S-O-M-E.*
- Spell **explorers.** Get ready. (Signal.) *E-X-P-L-O-R-E-R-S.*
- Spell **discovered.** Get ready. (Signal.) *D-I-S-C-O-V-E-R-E-D.*
- Spell **treasure.** Get ready. (Signal.) *T-R-E-A-S-U-R-E.*
- Spell **magic.** Get ready. (Signal.) *M-A-G-I-C.*
- Spell **island.** Get ready. (Signal.) *I-S-L-A-N-D.*

EXERCISE 3

Spelling Review

a. You're going to write words.
- Number your paper from 1 to 6. ✔
b. Word 1 is **saddest.** Write it. ✔
c. Word 2 is **saltiest.** Write it. ✔
d. (Repeat step c for: **3. science, 4. dangerous, 5. reception, 6. settlement.**)
e. Check your work. Make an **X** next to any word you got wrong.
f. Word 1. Spell **saddest.** Get ready. (Tap for each letter.) *S-A-D-D-E-S-T.*
- (Repeat for: **2. saltiest, 3. science, 4. dangerous, 5. reception, 6. settlement.**)

EXERCISE 1

Morphographic Analysis

a. (Write on the board:)

> 1. approval = _____ + _____ + _____
> 2. musical = _____ + _____ + _____
> 3. dishonesty = _____ + _____ + _____
> 4. intention = _____ + _____ + _____
> 5. speediest = _____ + _____ + _____
> 6. increasing = _____ + _____ + _____

- Copy the board. ✔
- Write the morphographs in each word after the equal sign. Put plus signs between the morphographs. ✔

b. (Change the board to show:)

> 1. approval = ap + prove + al
> 2. musical = muse + ic + al
> 3. dishonesty = dis + honest + y
> 4. intention = in + tent + ion
> 5. speediest = speed + y + est
> 6. increasing = in + crease + ing

c. Check your work. Make an **X** next to any word you got wrong.

EXERCISE 2

Sentence

a. You're going to write this sentence: **Some explorers discovered treasure on a magic island.**

b. Say the sentence. Get ready. (Signal.) *Some explorers discovered treasure on a magic island.*

c. Write the sentence. ✔

d. (Write on the board:)

> **Some explorers discovered treasure on a magic island.**

e. Check your work. Make an **X** next to any word you got wrong. ✔

EXERCISE 3

Spelling Review

a. Get ready to spell words.

b. Word 1 is **development**.
- What word? (Signal.) *Development.*
- Spell **development**. Get ready. (Signal.) *D-E-V-E-L-O-P-M-E-N-T.*

c. Word 2 is **transaction**.
- What word? (Signal.) *Transaction.*
- Spell **transaction**. Get ready. (Signal.) *T-R-A-N-S-A-C-T-I-O-N.*

d. (Repeat step c for: **3. childishly, 4. courage, 5. nervousness, 6. progression.**)

e. (Give individual turns on: **1. development, 2. transaction, 3. childishly, 4. courage, 5. nervousness, 6. progression.**)

EXERCISE 1

Affix Introduction

a. (Write on the board:)

> 1. sub + ject =
> 2. sub + merge =
> 3. sub + scribe =

- All these words have the morphograph **sub.**
b. Number your paper from 1 to 3. ✔
c. Add the morphographs together to make new words. Write just the new words. ✔
d. Check your work. Make an **X** next to any word you got wrong.
e. Word 1. Spell **subject.** Get ready. (Tap for each letter.) *S-U-B-J-E-C-T.*
- (Repeat for: **2. submerge, 3. subscribe.**)

EXERCISE 2

Word Building

a. (Write on the board:)

> 1. know + en = _____
> 2. for + give + ing = _____
> 3. pre + tend + ed = _____
> 4. ripe + en + ing = _____
> 5. brief + ly = _____
> 6. in + act + ion = _____

b. You're going to write the words that go in the blanks.
- Number your paper from 1 to 6. ✔
c. Word 1. Write **known** on your paper. ✔
d. Do the rest of the words on your own. ✔
e. Check your work. Make an **X** next to any word you got wrong.
f. Word 1. Spell **known.** Get ready. (Tap for each letter.) *K-N-O-W-N.*
- (Repeat for: **2. forgiving, 3. pretended, 4. ripening, 5. briefly, 6. inaction.**)

EXERCISE 3

Prompted Review

a. (Write on the board:)

> 1. known
> 2. treasure
> 3. straighten
> 4. intensively
> 5. requested
> 6. conquests

b. Word 1 is **known.** Spell **known.** Get ready. (Signal.) *K-N-O-W-N.*
c. Word 2 is **treasure.** Spell **treasure.** Get ready. (Signal.) *T-R-E-A-S-U-R-E.*
d. (Repeat step c for: **3. straighten, 4. intensively, 5. requested, 6. conquests.**)
e. (Erase the board.)
- Now spell those words without looking.
f. Word 1 is **known.** Spell **known.** Get ready. (Signal.) *K-N-O-W-N.*
g. Word 2 is **treasure.** Spell **treasure.** Get ready. (Signal.) *T-R-E-A-S-U-R-E.*
h. (Repeat step g for: **3. straighten, 4. intensively, 5. requested, 6. conquests.**)
i. (Give individual turns on: **1. known, 2. treasure, 3. straighten, 4. intensively, 5. requested, 6. conquests.**)

EXERCISE 1

Nonword Base

a. (Write on the board:)

> **struct**

- One morphograph that cannot stand alone is **struct**.
- What morphograph? (Signal.) *Struct.*
- Spell **struct**. Get ready. (Signal.) *S-T-R-U-C-T.*

b. Get ready to spell words that have the morphograph **struct**.

c. First word: **destruction**.

- What's the first morphograph in **destruction?** (Signal.) *De.*
- Next morphograph? (Signal.) *Struct.*
- Next morphograph? (Signal.) *Ion.*
- Spell **destruction**. Get ready. (Signal.) *D-E-S-T-R-U-C-T-I-O-N.*

d. Next word: **construct**.

- What's the first morphograph in **construct?** (Signal.) *Con.*
- Next morphograph? (Signal.) *Struct.*
- Spell **construct**. Get ready. (Signal.) *C-O-N-S-T-R-U-C-T.*

e. (For **structure** and **instruct**, have students identify each morphograph and spell each entire word.)

EXERCISE 2

Morphographic Analysis

a. (Write on the board:)

> 1. subjective =
> 2. forgiven =
> 3. contended =
> 4. appraisal =
> 5. transported =
> 6. provision =

- Copy the board. ✔
- Write the three morphographs in each word after the equal sign. Put plus signs between the morphographs. ✔

b. (Change the board to show:)

> 1. subjective = sub + ject + ive
> 2. forgiven = for + give + en
> 3. contended = con + tend + ed
> 4. appraisal = ap + praise + al
> 5. transported = trans + port + ed
> 6. provision = pro + vise + ion

c. Check your work. Make an **X** next to any word you got wrong.

EXERCISE 3

Prompted Review

a. (Write on the board:)

> 1. islands
> 2. blown
> 3. subscribed
> 4. medic
> 5. production
> 6. explorers

b. Word 1 is **islands**. Spell **islands**. Get ready. (Signal.) *I-S-L-A-N-D-S.*

c. Word 2 is **blown**. Spell **blown**. Get ready. (Signal.) *B-L-O-W-N.*

d. (Repeat step c for: **3. subscribed, 4. medic, 5. production, 6. explorers.**)

e. (Erase the board.)

- Now spell those words without looking.

f. Word 1 is **islands**. Spell **islands**. Get ready. (Signal.) *I-S-L-A-N-D-S.*

g. Word 2 is **blown**. Spell **blown**. Get ready. (Signal.) *B-L-O-W-N.*

h. (Repeat step g for: **3. subscribed, 4. medic, 5. production, 6. explorers.**)

i. (Give individual turns on: **1. islands, 2. blown, 3. subscribed, 4. medic, 5. production, 6. explorers.**)

LESSON 77

EXERCISE 1

Affix Introduction

a. (Write on the board:)

> 1. ob + serve =
> 2. ob + tain =
> 3. ob + ject =

- All these words have the morphograph **ob.**
b. Number your paper from 1 to 3. ✔
c. Add the morphographs together to make new words. Write just the new words. ✔
d. Check your work. Make an **X** next to any word you got wrong.
e. Word 1. Spell **observe.** Get ready. (Tap for each letter.) *O-B-S-E-R-V-E.*
- (Repeat for: **2. obtain, 3. object.**)

EXERCISE 2

Word Building

a. (Write on the board:)

> 1. fine + ish = _____
> 2. de + sign + er = _____
> 3. simple + est = _____
> 4. un + re + vise + ed = _____
> 5. pup + y + es = _____
> 6. comic + al = _____

b. You're going to write the words that go in the blanks.
- Number your paper from 1 to 6. ✔
c. Word 1. Write **finish** on your paper. ✔
d. Do the rest of the words on your own. ✔
e. Check your work. Make an **X** next to any word you got wrong.
f. Word 1. Spell **finish.** Get ready. (Tap for each letter.) *F-I-N-I-S-H.*
- (Repeat for: **2. designer, 3. simplest, 4. unrevised, 5. puppies, 6. comical.**)

EXERCISE 3

Spelling Review

a. Get ready to spell words.
b. Word 1 is **unknown.**
- What word? (Signal.) *Unknown.*
- Spell **unknown.** Get ready. (Signal.) *U-N-K-N-O-W-N.*
c. Word 2 is **instruction.**
- What word? (Signal.) *Instruction.*
- Spell **instruction.** Get ready. (Signal.) *I-N-S-T-R-U-C-T-I-O-N.*
d. (Repeat step c for: **3. subscribed, 4. unproven, 5. pretending, 6. briefest.**)
e. (Give individual turns on: **1. unknown 2. instruction, 3. subscribed, 4. unproven, 5. pretending, 6. briefest.**)

<hr>

EXERCISE 1

Nonword Base

a. (Write on the board:)

> **tract**

- One morphograph that combines with other morphographs is **tract.**
- What morphograph? (Signal.) *Tract.*
- Spell **tract.** Get ready. (Signal.) *T-R-A-C-T.*

b. Get ready to spell words that have the morphograph **tract.**

c. First word: **contract.**

- What's the first morphograph in **contract?** (Signal.) *Con.*
- Next morphograph? (Signal.) *Tract.*
- Spell **contract.** Get ready. (Signal.) *C-O-N-T-R-A-C-T.*

d. Next word: **extract.**

- What's the first morphograph in **extract?** (Signal.) *Ex.*
- Next morphograph? (Signal.) *Tract.*
- Spell **extract.** Get ready. (Signal.) *E-X-T-R-A-C-T.*

e. (For **traction** and **subtract,** have students identify each morphograph and spell each entire word.)

<hr>

EXERCISE 2

Sentence Variation

a. Get ready to write on lined paper.

- You are going to write a sentence made up of words you know how to spell. Put the right punctuation mark at the end of the sentence.

b. The sentence is **Some scientists discovered an injection to increase health and strength.**

- Say that sentence. Get ready. (Signal.) *Some scientists discovered an injection to increase health and strength.*
- (Repeat until firm.)

c. Write it. ✔

d. Get ready to check your spelling. Put an **X** next to any word you missed.

e. Spell **Some.** Get ready. (Signal.) *S-O-M-E.*

- Check it. ✔

f. Spell **scientists.** Get ready. (Signal.) *S-C-I-E-N-T-I-S-T-S.*

- Check it. ✔
- (Repeat for: **discovered, injection, increase, health, strength.**)

g. What end mark did you put at the end of the sentence? (Signal.) *A period.*

- Check it. ✔

h. Fix any words you missed.

<hr>

EXERCISE 3

Prompted Review

a. (Write on the board:)

> 1. objection
> 2. destructive
> 3. forgiving
> 4. honesty
> 5. prevention
> 6. readily

b. Word 1 is **objection.** Spell **objection.** Get ready. (Signal.) *O-B-J-E-C-T-I-O-N.*

c. Word 2 is **destructive.** Spell **destructive.** Get ready. (Signal.) *D-E-S-T-R-U-C-T-I-V-E.*

d. (Repeat step c for: **3. forgiving, 4. honesty, 5. prevention, 6. readily.**)

e. (Erase the board.)

- Now spell those words without looking.

f. Word 1 is **objection.** Spell **objection.** Get ready. (Signal.) *O-B-J-E-C-T-I-O-N.*

g. Word 2 is **destructive.** Spell **destructive.** Get ready. (Signal.) *D-E-S-T-R-U-C-T-I-V-E.*

h. (Repeat step g for: **3. forgiving, 4. honesty, 5. prevention, 6. readily.**)

i. (Give individual turns on: **1. objection, 2. destructive, 3. forgiving, 4. honesty, 5. prevention, 6. readily.**)

EXERCISE 1

Word Introduction

a. (Write on the board:)

> pound
> habit
> saint
> brother
> sister
> false

b. Get ready to read these words.
- First word: **pound.** What word? (Signal.)
  Pound.
c. Next word: **habit.** What word? (Signal.)
  Habit.
- (Repeat for: **saint, brother, sister, false.**)
d. Now spell those words.
- Spell **pound.** Get ready. (Signal.)
  P-O-U-N-D.
e. Spell **habit.** Get ready. (Signal.) *H-A-B-I-T.*
- (Repeat for: **saint, brother, sister, false.**)
f. (Erase the board.)
- Spell the words without looking.
g. Spell **pound.** Get ready. (Signal.)
  P-O-U-N-D.
h. Spell **habit.** Get ready. (Signal.) *H-A-B-I-T.*
- (Repeat for: **saint, brother, sister, false.**)
i. Get ready to write those words.
j. First word: **pound.** Write it. ✔
- (Repeat for: **habit, saint, brother, sister, false.**)

EXERCISE 2

Morphographic Analysis

a. (Write on the board:)

> 1. retraction = ____ + ____ + ____
> 2. madness = ____ + ____
> 3. construction = ____ + ____ + ____
> 4. furious = ____ + ____
> 5. misstatement = ____ + ____ + ____
> 6. exposure = ____ + ____ + ____

- Copy the board. ✔
- Write the morphographs in each word after the equal sign. Put plus signs between the morphographs. ✔

b. (Change the board to show:)

> 1. **retraction =** re + tract + ion
> 2. **madness =** mad + ness
> 3. **construction =** con + struct + ion
> 4. **furious =** fury + ous
> 5. **misstatement =** mis + state + ment
> 6. **exposure =** ex + pose + ure

c. Check your work. Make an **X** next to any word you got wrong.

EXERCISE 3

Spelling Review

a. You're going to write words.
- Number your paper from 1 to 6. ✔
b. Word 1 is **consignment.** Write it.
c. Word 2 is **photographer.** Write it.
d. (Repeat step c for: **3. unstretched, 4. tries, 5. unfriendliest, 6. unfashionable.**)
e. Check your work. Make an **X** next to any word you got wrong.
f. Word 1. Spell **consignment.** Get ready. (Tap for each letter.)
  C-O-N-S-I-G-N-M-E-N-T.
- (Repeat for: **2. photographer, 3. unstretched, 4. tries, 5. unfriendliest, 6. unfashionable.**)

LESSON 80

EXERCISE 1

Test

a. Today you have a spelling test. Number your lined paper from 1 through 10. ✔

b. Word 1 is **chiefly.** What word? (Signal.) *Chiefly.*

• Write the word **chiefly.** ✔

c. Word 2 is **treasure.** What word? (Signal.) *Treasure.*

• Write the word **treasure.** ✔

d. Word 3 is **science.** What word? (Signal.) *Science.*

• Write the word **science.** ✔

e. Word 4 is **inspection.** What word? (Signal.) *Inspection.*

• Write the word **inspection.** ✔

f. Word 5 is **protective.** What word? (Signal.) *Protective.*

• Write the word **protective.** ✔

g. Word 6 is **exposure.** What word? (Signal.) *Exposure.*

• Write the word **exposure.** ✔

h. Word 7 is **pretending.** What word? (Signal.) *Pretending.*

• Write the word **pretending.** ✔

i. Word 8 is **structure.** What word? (Signal.) *Structure.*

• Write the word **structure.** ✔

j. Word 9 is **objection.** What word? (Signal.) *Objection.*

• Write the word **objection.** ✔

k. Word 10 is **creatively.** What word? (Signal.) *Creatively.*

• Write the word **creatively.** ✔

l. Pick up your red pen. ✔
Make an **X** next to any word you spelled wrong.

• (Write on the board:)

1. chiefly	6. exposure
2. treasure	7. pretending
3. science	8. structure
4. inspection	9. objection
5. protective	10. creatively

• Write the correct spelling next to any word you spelled wrong.
(Observe students and give feedback.)

EXERCISE 1

Affix Introduction

a. (Write on the board:)

> 1. fact + ual =
> 2. grade + ual =
> 3. use + ual =

- All these words have the morphograph **ual.**
b. Number your paper from 1 to 3. ✔
c. Add the morphographs together to make new words. Write just the new words. ✔
d. Check your work. Make an **X** next to any word you got wrong.
e. Word 1. Spell **factual.** Get ready. (Tap for each letter.) *F-A-C-T-U-A-L.*
- (Repeat for: **2. gradual, 3. usual.**)

EXERCISE 2

Word Building

a. (Write on the board:)

> 1. in + cure + able = _____
> 2. brother + ly = _____
> 3. sub + tract + ion = _____
> 4. ob + ject + ive = _____
> 5. in + struct + ion = _____
> 6. sub + ject + ive = _____

b. You're going to write the words that go in the blanks.
- Number your paper from 1 to 6. ✔
c. Word 1. Write **incurable** on your paper. ✔
d. Do the rest of the words on your own. ✔
e. Check your work. Make an **X** next to any word you got wrong.
f. Word 1. Spell **incurable.** Get ready. (Tap for each letter.) *I-N-C-U-R-A-B-L-E.*
- (Repeat for: **2. brotherly, 3. subtraction, 4. objective, 5. instruction, 6. subjective.**)

EXERCISE 3

Prompted Review

a. (Write on the board:)

> 1. island
> 2. drawn
> 3. rejection
> 4. sister
> 5. subscriber
> 6. unforgiving

b. Word 1 is **island.** Spell **island.** Get ready. (Signal.) *I-S-L-A-N-D.*
c. Word 2 is **drawn.** Spell **drawn.** Get ready. (Signal.) *D-R-A-W-N.*
d. (Repeat step c for: **3. rejection, 4. sister, 5. subscriber, 6. unforgiving.**)
e. (Erase the board.)
- Now spell those words without looking.
f. Word 1 is **island.** Spell **island.** Get ready. (Signal.) *I-S-L-A-N-D.*
g. Word 2 is **drawn.** Spell **drawn.** Get ready. (Signal.) *D-R-A-W-N.*
h. (Repeat step g for: **3. rejection, 4. sister, 5. subscriber, 6. unforgiving.**)
i. (Give individual turns on: **1. island, 2. drawn, 3. rejection, 4. sister, 5. subscriber, 6. unforgiving.**)

LESSON 82

EXERCISE 1

Nonword Base

a. (Write on the board:)

> **sist**

- One morphograph that cannot stand alone is **sist.**
- What morphograph? (Signal.) *Sist.*
- Spell **sist.** Get ready. (Signal.) *S-I-S-T.*

b. Get ready to spell words that have the morphograph **sist.**

c. First word: **insist.**
- What's the first morphograph in **insist?** (Signal.) *In.*
- Next morphograph? (Signal.) *Sist.*
- Spell **insist.** Get ready. (Signal.) *I-N-S-I-S-T.*

d. Next word: **resist.**
- What's the first morphograph in **resist?** (Signal.) *Re.*
- Next morphograph? (Signal.) *Sist.*
- Spell **resist.** Get ready. (Signal.) *R-E-S-I-S-T.*

e. (For **consist** and **subsist,** have students identify each morphograph and spell each entire word.)

EXERCISE 2

Sentence

a. (Write on the board:)

> **That student appears to be thorough and conscientious.**

- I'll read the sentence on the board. **That student appears to be thorough and conscientious.**
- Let's spell some of those words.

b. Spell **That.** Get ready. (Signal.) *T-H-A-T.*
- Spell **student.** Get ready. (Signal.) *S-T-U-D-E-N-T.*
- Spell **appears.** Get ready. (Signal.) *A-P-P-E-A-R-S.*
- Spell **thorough.** Get ready. (Signal.) *T-H-O-R-O-U-G-H.*
- Spell **conscientious.** Get ready. (Signal.) *C-O-N-S-C-I-E-N-T-I-O-U-S.*

c. Copy this sentence on lined paper.

d. (Pause, then check and correct.)
- Read the sentence you just copied. Get ready. (Signal.) *That student appears to be thorough and conscientious.*

EXERCISE 3

Spelling Review

a. You're going to write words.
- Number your paper from 1 to 6. ✔

b. Word 1 is **pretended.** Write it. ✔

c. Word 2 is **tomorrow.** Write it. ✔

d. (Repeat Step c for: **3. courage, 4. creative, 5. exposure, 6. dishonestly.**)

e. Check your work. Make an **X** next to any word you got wrong.

f. Word 1. Spell **pretended.** Get ready. (Tap for each letter.) *P-R-E-T-E-N-D-E-D.*
- (Repeat for: **2. tomorrow, 3. courage, 4. creative, 5. exposure, 6. dishonestly.**)

EXERCISE 1

Affix Introduction

a. (Write on the board:)

> 1. per + form =
> 2. per + tain =
> 3. per + cept + ion =

• All these words have the morphograph **per.**

b. Number your paper from 1 to 3. ✔

c. Add the morphographs together to make new words. Write just the new words. ✔

d. Check your work. Make an **X** next to any word you got wrong.

e. Word 1. Spell **perform.** Get ready. (Tap for each letter.) *P-E-R-F-O-R-M.*

• (Repeat for: **2. pertain, 3. perception.**)

EXERCISE 2

Sentence

a. (Write on the board:)

> That student appears to be thorough and conscientious.

• I'll read the sentence on the board. **That student appears to be thorough and conscientious.**

• Let's spell some of those words.

b. Spell **That.** Get ready. (Signal.) *T-H-A-T.*

• Spell **student.** Get ready. (Signal.) *S-T-U-D-E-N-T.*

• Spell **appears.** Get ready. (Signal.) *A-P-P-E-A-R-S.*

• Spell **thorough.** Get ready. (Signal.) *T-H-O-R-O-U-G-H.*

• Spell **conscientious.** Get ready. (Signal.) *C-O-N-S-C-I-E-N-T-I-O-U-S.*

c. (Erase the board.)

d. Now let's spell some of the words in that sentence without looking.

• Spell **That.** Get ready. (Signal.) *T-H-A-T.*

• Spell **student.** Get ready. (Signal.) *S-T-U-D-E-N-T.*

• Spell **appears.** Get ready. (Signal.) *A-P-P-E-A-R-S.*

• Spell **thorough.** Get ready. (Signal.) *T-H-O-R-O-U-G-H.*

• Spell **conscientious.** Get ready. (Signal.) *C-O-N-S-C-I-E-N-T-I-O-U-S.*

EXERCISE 3

Prompted Review

a. (Write on the board:)

> 1. consisted
> 2. intention
> 3. retraction
> 4. shown
> 5. matches
> 6. factual

b. Word 1 is **consisted.** Spell **consisted.** Get ready. (Signal.) *C-O-N-S-I-S-T-E-D.*

c. Word 2 is **intention.** Spell **intention.** Get ready. (Signal.) *I-N-T-E-N-T-I-O-N.*

d. (Repeat step c for: **3. retraction, 4. shown, 5. matches, 6. factual.**)

e. (Erase the board.)

• Now spell those words without looking.

f. Word 1 is **consisted.** Spell **consisted.** Get ready. (Signal.) *C-O-N-S-I-S-T-E-D.*

g. Word 2 is **intention.** Spell **intention.** Get ready. (Signal.) *I-N-T-E-N-T-I-O-N.*

h. (Repeat step g for: **3. retraction, 4. shown, 5. matches, 6. factual.**)

i. (Give individual turns on: **1. consisted, 2. intention, 3. retraction, 4. shown, 5. matches, 6. factual.**)

EXERCISE 1

A-L Insertion

a. Here is a new rule for words that end in **i-c.**
- Listen: When the word ends in the letters **i-c,** you must add the morphograph **a-l** before adding **l-y.**
- Listen again: When the word ends in the letters **i-c,** you must add the morphograph **a-l** before adding **l-y.**

b. Everybody, tell me when you add **a-l** before **l-y.** (Pause.) Get ready. (Signal.) *When the word ends in the letters i-c.*
- (Repeat until firm.)

c. (Write on the board:)

> **1. magic**
>
> **2. basic**
>
> **3. critic**

- What letters do these words end in? (Signal.) *I-C.*

d. (Point to **magic.**)
- So if we write the word **magically,** what morphograph must we add before the **l-y?** (Signal.) *A-L.*

e. (Write **+ al** after **magic:**)

> **1. magic + al**

- Now we add **l-y.**
- (Write **+ ly** after **magic + al:**)

> **1. magic + al + ly**

f. Everybody, spell **magically.** Get ready. (Signal.) *M-A-G-I-C-A-L-L-Y.*

g. (Point to **basic.**)
- What letters does **basic** end in? (Signal.) *I-C.*
- So what morphograph would we add before the **l-y** in **basically?** (Signal.) *A-L.*

h. Everybody, spell **basically.** Get ready. (Signal.) *B-A-S-I-C-A-L-L-Y.*

i. (Point to **critic.**)
- What letters does **critic** end in? (Signal.) *I-C.*
- So what morphograph would we add before the **l-y** in **critically?** (Signal.) *A-L.*

j. Everybody, spell **critically.** Get ready. (Signal.) *C-R-I-T-I-C-A-L-L-Y.*

k. (Give individual turns on: **magically, basically,** and **critically.**)

EXERCISE 2

Sentence

a. (Write on the board:)

> **That student appears to be thorough and conscientious.**

- I'll read the sentence on the board. **That student appears to be thorough and conscientious.**
- Let's spell some of those words.

b. Spell **That.** Get ready. (Signal.) *T-H-A-T.*
- Spell **student.** Get ready. (Signal.) *S-T-U-D-E-N-T.*
- Spell **appears.** Get ready. (Signal.) *A-P-P-E-A-R-S.*
- Spell **thorough.** Get ready. (Signal.) *T-H-O-R-O-U-G-H.*
- Spell **conscientious.** Get ready. (Signal.) *C-O-N-S-C-I-E-N-T-I-O-U-S.*

c. (Erase the board.)

d. Now let's spell some of the words in that sentence without looking.
- Spell **That.** Get ready. (Signal.) *T-H-A-T.*
- Spell **student.** Get ready. (Signal.) *S-T-U-D-E-N-T.*
- Spell **appears.** Get ready. (Signal.) *A-P-P-E-A-R-S.*
- Spell **thorough.** Get ready. (Signal.) *T-H-O-R-O-U-G-H.*
- Spell **conscientious.** Get ready. (Signal.) *C-O-N-S-C-I-E-N-T-I-O-U-S.*

Sentence Variation

a. Get ready to write on lined paper.
- You are going to write a sentence made up of words you know how to spell. Put the right punctuation mark at the end of the sentence.

b. The sentence is **She discovered her physical protection was doubtful.**
- Say that sentence. Get ready. (Signal.) *She discovered her physical protection was doubtful.*
- (Repeat until firm.)

c. Write it. ✔

d. Get ready to check your spelling. Put an **X** next to any word you missed.

e. Spell **She.** Get ready. (Signal.) *S-H-E.*
- Check it. ✔

f. Spell **discovered.** Get ready. (Signal.) *D-I-S-C-O-V-E-R-E-D.*
- Check it. ✔
- (Repeat for: **her, physical, protection, was, doubtful.**)

g. What punctuation mark did you put at the end of the sentence? (Signal.) *A period.*
- Check it. ✔

h. Fix any words you missed.

LESSON 85

EXERCISE 1

A-L Insertion

a. Everybody, tell me when you add **a-l** before **l-y.** (Pause.) Get ready. (Signal.) *When the word ends in the letters i-c.*

• (Repeat until firm.)

b. (Write on the board:)

> 1. critic + ly =
>
> 2. cost + ly =
>
> 3. heroic + ly =
>
> 4. magic + ly =
>
> 5. firm + ly =
>
> 6. rhythmic + ly =
>
> 7. chief + ly =
>
> 8. comic + ly =

c. Copy the board to your paper, and then add the endings. Remember the rule about adding **a-l** before **l-y.** ✔

d. I'll spell each word.

• Put an **X** next to any word you missed and write that word correctly.

• (Spell each word twice. Write the words on the board as you spell them.)

> 1. critic + ly = critically
>
> 2. cost + ly = costly
>
> 3. heroic + ly = heroically
>
> 4. magic + ly = magically
>
> 5. firm + ly = firmly
>
> 6. rhythmic + ly = rhythmically
>
> 7. chief + ly = chiefly
>
> 8. comic + ly = comically

EXERCISE 2

Sentence

a. You're going to write this sentence. **That student appears to be thorough and conscientious.**

b. Say the sentence. Get ready. (Signal.) *That student appears to be thorough and conscientious.*

c. Write the sentence. ✔

d. (Write on the board:)

> **That student appears to be thorough and conscientious.**

e. Check your work. Make an **X** next to any word you got wrong. ✔

EXERCISE 3

Spelling Review

a. Get ready to spell words.

b. Word 1 is **pertain.**

• What word? (Signal.) *Pertain.*

• Spell **pertain.** Get ready. (Signal.) *P-E-R-T-A-I-N.*

c. Word 2 is **insisted.**

• What word? (Signal.) *Insisted.*

• Spell **insisted.** Get ready. (Signal.) *I-N-S-I-S-T-E-D.*

d. (Repeat step c for: **3. bodies, 4. spinners, 5. unknown, 6. instead.**)

e. (Give individual turns on: **1. pertain, 2. insisted, 3. bodies, 4. spinners, 5. unknown, 6. instead.**)

LESSON 86

EXERCISE 1

Affix Introduction

> *Note:* Pronounce the morphograph **a** as the first sound in alike: **uh.**

a. (Write on the board:)

> 1. a + like =
> 2. a + part =
> 3. a + round =

- All these words have the morphograph **a.**
b. Number your paper from 1 to 3. ✔
c. Add the morphographs together to make new words. Write just the new words. ✔
d. Check your work. Make an **X** next to any word you got wrong.
e. Word 1. Spell **alike.** Get ready. (Tap for each letter.) *A-L-I-K-E.*
- (Repeat for: **2. apart, 3. around.**)

EXERCISE 2

Word Building

a. (Write on the board:)

> 1. con + vent + ion = _____
> 2. grade + ual = _____
> 3. tract + ion = _____
> 4. ob + ject + ive = _____
> 5. per + cept + ion = _____
> 6. re + sist + ing = _____

b. You're going to write the words that go in the blanks.
- Number your paper from 1 to 6. ✔
c. Word 1. Write **convention** on your paper. ✔
d. Do the rest of the words on your own. ✔
e. Check your work. Make an **X** next to any word you got wrong.
f. Word 1. Spell **convention.** Get ready. (Tap for each letter.) *C-O-N-V-E-N-T-I-O-N.*
- (Repeat for: **2. gradual, 3. traction, 4. objective, 5. perception, 6. resisting.**)

EXERCISE 3

Prompted Review

a. (Write on the board:)

> 1. assistants
> 2. heroically
> 3. perceptive
> 4. subscriber
> 5. conscientious
> 6. thorough

b. Word 1 is **assistants.** Spell **assistants.** Get ready. (Signal.) *A-S-S-I-S-T-A-N-T-S.*
c. Word 2 is **heroically.** Spell **heroically.** Get ready. (Signal.) *H-E-R-O-I-C-A-L-L-Y.*
d. (Repeat step c for: **3. perceptive, 4. subscriber, 5. conscientious, 6. thorough.**)
e. (Erase the board.)
- Now spell those words without looking.
f. Word 1 is **assistants.** Spell **assistants.** Get ready. (Signal.) *A-S-S-I-S-T-A-N-T-S.*
g. Word 2 is **heroically.** Spell **heroically.** Get ready. (Signal.) *H-E-R-O-I-C-A-L-L-Y.*
h. (Repeat step g for: **3. perceptive, 4. subscriber, 5. conscientious, 6. thorough.**)
i. (Give individual turns on: **1. assistants, 2. heroically, 3. perceptive, 4. subscriber, 5. conscientious, 6. thorough.**)

LESSON 87

EXERCISE 1

Nonword Base

a. (Write on the board:)

> **fect**

- One morphograph that cannot stand alone is **fect.**
- What morphograph? (Signal.) *Fect.*
- Spell **fect.** Get ready. (Signal.) *F-E-C-T.*

b. Get ready to spell words that have the morphograph **fect.**

c. First word: **defective.**
- What's the first morphograph in **defective?** (Signal.) *De.*
- Next morphograph? (Signal.) *Fect.*
- Next morphograph? (Signal.) *Ive.*
- Spell **defective.** Get ready. (Signal.) *D-E-F-E-C-T-I-V-E.*

d. Next word: **infect.**
- What's the first morphograph in **infect?** (Signal.) *In.*
- Next morphograph? (Signal.) *Fect.*
- Spell **infect.** Get ready. (Signal.) *I-N-F-E-C-T.*

e. (For **perfect,** have students identify each morphograph and spell the entire word.)

EXERCISE 2

Morphographic Analysis

a. (Write on the board:)

> 1. **usual** = _____ + _____
> 2. **apartment** = _____ + _____ + _____
> 3. **unrevised** = ___ + ___ + ___ + ___
> 4. **extended** = _____ + _____ + _____
> 5. **musical** = _____ + _____ + _____
> 6. **translation** = _____ + _____ + _____

- Copy the board. ✔
- Write the morphographs in each word after the equal sign. Put plus signs between the morphographs. ✔

b. (Change the board to show:)

> 1. **usual** = use + ual
> 2. **apartment** = a + part + ment
> 3. **unrevised** = un + re + vise + ed
> 4. **extended** = ex + tend + ed
> 5. **musical** = muse + ic + al
> 6. **translation** = trans + late + ion

c. Check your work. Make an **X** next to any word you got wrong.

EXERCISE 3

Spelling Review

a. You're going to write words.
- Number your paper from 1 to 6. ✔

b. Word 1 is **shown.** Write it.

c. Word 2 is **gradual.** Write it.

d. (Repeat step c for: **3. critically, 4. appears, 5. subtraction, 6. production.**)

e. Check your work. Make an **X** next to any word you got wrong.

f. Word 1. Spell **shown.** Get ready. (Tap for each letter.) *S-H-O-W-N.*
- (Repeat for: **2. gradual, 3. critically, 4. appears, 5. subtraction, 6. production.**)

EXERCISE 1

Affix Introduction

a. (Write on the board:)

> **1. com + pose =**
> **2. com + press =**
> **3. com + plain =**

• All these words have the morphograph **com.**

b. Number your paper from 1 to 3. ✔

c. Add the morphographs together to make new words. Write just the new words. ✔

d. Check your work. Make an **X** next to any word you got wrong.

e. Word 1. Spell **compose.** Get ready. (Tap for each letter.) *C-O-M-P-O-S-E.*

• (Repeat for: **2. compress, 3. complain.**)

EXERCISE 2

Word Building

a. (Write on the board:)

> **1. in + fect + ion =** _____
> **2. per + form + ing =** _____
> **3. con + sist + ed =** _____
> **4. fact + ual + ly =** _____
> **5. sphere + ic + al =** _____
> **6. con + tent + ment =** _____

b. You're going to write the words that go in the blanks.

• Number your paper from 1 to 6. ✔

c. Word 1. Write **infection** on your paper. ✔

d. Do the rest of the words on your own. ✔

e. Check your work. Make an **X** next to any word you got wrong.

f. Word 1. Spell **infection.** Get ready. (Tap for each letter.) *I-N-F-E-C-T-I-O-N.*

• (Repeat for: **2. performing, 3. consisted, 4. factually, 5. spherical, 6. contentment.**)

EXERCISE 3

Prompted Review

a. (Write on the board:)

> **1. thorough**
> **2. compression**
> **3. discovered**
> **4. rhythmically**
> **5. unusual**
> **6. automobile**

b. Word 1 is **thorough.** Spell **thorough.** Get ready. (Signal.) *T-H-O-R-O-U-G-H.*

c. Word 2 is **compression.** Spell **compression.** Get ready. (Signal.) *C-O-M-P-R-E-S-S-I-O-N.*

d. (Repeat step c for: **3. discovered, 4. rhythmically, 5. unusual, 6. automobile.**)

e. (Erase the board.)

• Now spell those words without looking.

f. Word 1 is **thorough.** Spell **thorough.** Get ready. (Signal.) *T-H-O-R-O-U-G-H.*

g. Word 2 is **compression.** Spell **compression.** Get ready. (Signal.) *C-O-M-P-R-E-S-S-I-O-N.*

h. (Repeat step g for: **3. discovered, 4. rhythmically, 5. unusual, 6. automobile.**)

i. (Give individual turns on: **1. thorough, 2. compression, 3. discovered, 4. rhythmically, 5. unusual, 6. automobile.**)

EXERCISE 1

Nonword Base

> *Note:* Pronounce the morphograph **cur** as in current.

a. (Write on the board:)

cur

- One morphograph that cannot stand alone is **cur.**
- What morphograph? (Signal.) *Cur.*
- Spell **cur.** Get ready. (Signal.) *C-U-R.*

b. Get ready to spell words that have the morphograph **cur.**

c. First word: **recur.**

- What's the first morphograph in **recur?** (Signal.) *Re.*
- Next morphograph? (Signal.) *Cur.*
- Spell **recur.** Get ready. (Signal.) *R-E-C-U-R.*

d. Next word: **incur.**

- What's the first morphograph in **incur?** (Signal.) *In.*
- Next morphograph? (Signal.) *Cur.*
- Spell **incur.** Get ready. (Signal.) *I-N-C-U-R.*

e. (For **concur,** have students identify each morphograph and spell the entire word.)

EXERCISE 2

Morphographic Analysis

a. (Write on the board:)

> 1. thoroughly = _____ + _____
> 2. gradual = _____ + _____
> 3. compresses = ____ + ____ + ____
> 4. perfection = ____ + ____ + ____
> 5. objective = ____ + ____ + ____
> 6. submerged = ____ + ____ + ____

- Write the morphographs in each word after the equal sign. Put plus signs between the morphographs. ✔

b. (Change the board to show:)

> 1. **thoroughly** = thorough + ly
> 2. **gradual** = grade + ual
> 3. **compresses** = com + press + es
> 4. **perfection** = per + fect + ion
> 5. **objective** = ob + ject + ive
> 6. **submerged** = sub + merge + ed

c. Check your work. Make an **X** next to any word you got wrong.

EXERCISE 3

Spelling Review

a. You're going to write words.

- Number your paper from 1 to 6. ✔

b. Word 1 is **consist.** Write it. ✔

c. Word 2 is **nicely.** Write it. ✔

d. (Repeat step c for: **3. deferment, 4. repel, 5. transforming, 6. inventive.**)

e. Check your work. Make an **X** next to any word you got wrong.

f. Word 1. Spell **consist.** Get ready. (Tap for each letter.) *C-O-N-S-I-S-T.*

- (Repeat for: **2. nicely, 3. deferment, 4. repel, 5. transforming, 6. inventive.**)

LESSON 90

EXERCISE 1

Test

a. Today you have a spelling test. Number your lined paper from 1 through 10. ✔

b. Word 1 is **delightful.** What word? (Signal.) *Delightful.*

• Write the word **delightful.** ✔

c. Word 2 is **respectfully.** What word? (Signal.) *Respectfully.*

• Write the word **respectfully.** ✔

d. Word 3 is **perception.** What word? (Signal.) *Perception.*

• Write the word **perception.** ✔

e. Word 4 is **thorough.** What word? (Signal.) *Thorough.*

• Write the word **thorough.** ✔

f. Word 5 is **liveliness.** What word? (Signal.) *Liveliness.*

• Write the word **liveliness.** ✔

g. Word 6 is **approval.** What word? (Signal.) *Approval.*

• Write the word **approval.** ✔

h. Word 7 is **extended.** What word? (Signal.) *Extended.*

• Write the word **extended.** ✔

i. Word 8 is **disposable.** What word? (Signal.) *Disposable.*

• Write the word **disposable.** ✔

j. Word 9 is **forgiven.** What word? (Signal.) *Forgiven.*

• Write the word **forgiven.** ✔

k. Word 10 is **thrown.** What word? (Signal.) *Thrown.*

• Write the word **thrown.** ✔

l. Pick up your red pen. ✔

Make an **X** next to any word you spelled wrong.

• (Write on the board:)

1. delightful	6. approval
2. respectfully	7. extended
3. perception	8. disposable
4. thorough	9. forgiven
5. liveliness	10. thrown

• Write the correct spelling next to any word you spelled wrong.

(Observe students and give feedback.)

EXERCISE 1

Word Introduction

a. (Write on the board:)

> loaf
> calf
> half
> shelf
> wolf

b. Get ready to read these words.
- First word: **loaf.** What word? (Signal.) *Loaf.*
c. Next word: **calf.** What word? (Signal.) *Calf.*
- (Repeat for: **half, shelf, wolf.**)
d. Now spell those words.
- Spell **loaf.** Get ready. (Signal.) *L-O-A-F.*
e. Spell **calf.** Get ready. (Signal.) *C-A-L-F.*
- (Repeat for: **half, shelf, wolf.**)
f. (Erase the board.)
- Spell the words without looking.
g. Spell **loaf.** Get ready. (Signal.) *L-O-A-F.*
h. Spell **calf.** Get ready. (Signal.) *C-A-L-F.*
- (Repeat for: **half, shelf, wolf.**)
i. Get ready to write those words.
j. First word: **loaf.** Write it. ✔
- (Repeat for: **calf, half, shelf, wolf.**)

EXERCISE 2

Word Building

a. (Write on the board:)

> 1. com + press + ion = _____
> 2. in + fect + ion = _____
> 3. a + part + ment = _____
> 4. per + tain + ed = _____
> 5. in + sist + ed = _____
> 6. use + ual + ly = _____

b. You're going to write the words that go in the blanks.
- Number your paper from 1 to 6. ✔
c. Word 1. Write **compression** on your paper. ✔
d. Do the rest of the words on your own. ✔
e. Check your work. Make an **X** next to any word you got wrong.

f. Word 1. Spell **compression.** Get ready. (Tap for each letter.) *C-O-M-P-R-E-S-S-I-O-N.*
- (Repeat for: **2. infection, 3. apartment, 4. pertained, 5. insisted, 6. usually.**)

EXERCISE 3

Prompted Review

a. (Write on the board:)

> 1. critically
> 2. submerging
> 3. island
> 4. relative
> 5. reception
> 6. rhythmically

b. Word 1 is **critically.** Spell **critically.** Get ready. (Signal.) *C-R-I-T-I-C-A-L-L-Y.*
c. Word 2 is **submerging.** Spell **submerging.** Get ready. (Signal.) *S-U-B-M-E-R-G-I-N-G.*
d. (Repeat step c for: **3. island, 4. relative, 5. reception, 6. rhythmically.**)
e. (Erase the board.)
- Now spell those words without looking.
f. Word 1 is **critically.** Spell **critically.** Get ready. (Signal.) *C-R-I-T-I-C-A-L-L-Y.*
g. Word 2 is **submerging.** Spell **submerging.** Get ready. (Signal.) *S-U-B-M-E-R-G-I-N-G.*
h. (Repeat step g for: **3. island, 4. relative, 5. reception, 6. rhythmically.**)
i. (Give individual turns on: **1. critically, 2. submerging, 3. island, 4. relative, 5. reception, 6. rhythmically.**)

EXERCISE 1

Affix Introduction

a. (Write on the board:)

> 1. mother + hood =
> 2. boy + hood =
> 3. like + ly + hood =

- All these words have the morphograph **hood.**
b. Number your paper from 1 to 3. ✔
c. Add the morphographs together to make new words. Write just the new words. ✔
d. Check your work. Make an **X** next to any word you got wrong.
e. Word 1. Spell **motherhood.** Get ready. (Tap for each letter.) *M-O-T-H-E-R-H-O-O-D.*
- (Repeat for: **2. boyhood, 3. likelihood.**)

EXERCISE 2

Word Introduction

a. (Write on the board:)

> wife
> life
> self
> knife
> leaf

b. Get ready to read these words.
- First word: **wife.** What word? (Signal.) *Wife.*
c. Next word: **life.** What word? (Signal.) *Life.*
- (Repeat for: **self, knife, leaf.**)
d. Now spell those words.
- Spell **wife.** Get ready. (Signal.) *W-I-F-E.*
e. Spell **life.** Get ready. (Signal.) *L-I-F-E.*
- (Repeat for: **self, knife, leaf.**)
f. (Erase the board.)
- Spell the words without looking.
g. Spell **wife.** Get ready. (Signal.) *W-I-F-E.*
h. Spell **life.** Get ready. (Signal.) *L-I-F-E.*
- (Repeat for: **self, knife, leaf.**)
i. Get ready to write those words.
j. First word: **wife.** Write it. ✔
- (Repeat for: **life, self, knife, leaf.**)

EXERCISE 3

Spelling Review

a. You're going to write words.
- Number your paper from 1 to 6. ✔
b. Word 1 is **half.** Write it.
c. Word 2 is **repression.** Write it.
d. (Repeat step c for: **3. thoroughly, 4. thrown, 5. carriage, 6. musical.**)
e. Check your work. Make an **X** next to any word you got wrong.
f. Word 1. Spell **half.** Get ready. (Tap for each letter.) *H-A-L-F.*
- (Repeat for: **2. repression, 3. thoroughly, 4. thrown, 5. carriage, 6. musical.**)

EXERCISE 1

Nonword Base

a. (Write on the board:)

> **miss**

- One morphograph that combines with other morphographs is **miss.**
- What morphograph? (Signal.) *Miss.*
- Spell **miss.** Get ready. (Signal.) *M-I-S-S.*

b. Get ready to spell words that have the morphograph **miss.**

c. First word: **dismiss.**

- What's the first morphograph in **dismiss?** (Signal.) *Dis.*
- Next morphograph? (Signal.) *Miss.*
- Spell **dismiss.** Get ready. (Signal.) *D-I-S-M-I-S-S.*

d. Next word: **mission.**

- What's the first morphograph in **mission?** (Signal.) *Miss.*
- Next morphograph? (Signal.) *Ion.*
- Spell **mission.** Get ready. (Signal.) *M-I-S-S-I-O-N.*

e. (For **commission** and **permission,** have students identify each morphograph and spell each entire word.)

EXERCISE 2

Morphographic Analysis

a. (Write on the board:)

> 1. complaining =
> 2. likelihood =
> 3. dismissal =
> 4. contraction =
> 5. destructive =
> 6. shipping =

- Copy the board. ✔
- Write the morphographs in each word after the equal sign. Put plus signs between the morphographs. ✔

b. (Change the board to show:)

> 1. complaining = com + plain + ing
> 2. likelihood = like + ly + hood
> 3. dismissal = dis + miss + al
> 4. contraction = con + tract + ion
> 5. destructive = de + struct + ive
> 6. shipping = ship + ing

c. Check your work. Make an **X** next to any word you got wrong.

EXERCISE 3

Spelling Review

a. You're going to write words.

- Number your paper from 1 to 6. ✔

b. Word 1 is **resisted.** Write it.

c. Word 2 is **performer.** Write it.

d. (Repeat step c for: **3. objection, 4. instructional, 5. heroically, 6. treasure.**)

e. Check your work. Make an **X** next to any word you got wrong.

f. Word 1. Spell **resisted.** Get ready. (Tap for each letter.) *R-E-S-I-S-T-E-D.*

- (Repeat for: **2. performer, 3. objection, 4. instructional, 5. heroically, 6. treasure.**)

EXERCISE 1

Nonword Base

a. (Write on the board:)

> **mit**

- One morphograph that cannot stand alone is **mit.**
- What morphograph? (Signal.) *Mit.*
- Spell **mit.** Get ready. (Signal.) *M-I-T.*

b. Get ready to spell words that have the morphograph **mit.**

c. First word: **permit.**

- What's the first morphograph in **permit?** (Signal.) *Per.*
- Next morphograph? (Signal.) *Mit.*
- Spell **permit.** Get ready. (Signal.) *P-E-R-M-I-T.*

d. Next word: **transmit.**

- What's the first morphograph in **transmit?** (Signal.) *Trans.*
- Next morphograph? (Signal.) *Mit.*
- Spell **transmit.** Get ready. (Signal.) *T-R-A-N-S-M-I-T.*

e. (For **commit,** have students identify each morphograph and spell the entire word.)

EXERCISE 2

Sentence

a. (Write on the board:)

> **Their approach to acquiring knowledge fascinates me.**

- I'll read the sentence on the board. **Their approach to acquiring knowledge fascinates me.**
- Let's spell some of those words.

b. Spell **Their.** Get ready. (Signal.) *T-H-E-I-R.*

- Spell **approach.** Get ready. (Signal.) *A-P-P-R-O-A-C-H.*
- Spell **acquiring.** Get ready. (Signal.) *A-C-Q-U-I-R-I-N-G.*
- Spell **knowledge.** Get ready. (Signal.) *K-N-O-W-L-E-D-G-E.*
- Spell **fascinates.** Get ready. (Signal.) *F-A-S-C-I-N-A-T-E-S.*

c. Copy this sentence on lined paper.

d. (Pause, then check and correct.)

- Read the sentence you just copied. Get ready. (Signal.) *Their approach to acquiring knowledge fascinates me.*

EXERCISE 3

Prompted Review

a. (Write on the board:)

> 1. unlikeliest
> 2. mission
> 3. complained
> 4. accidentally
> 5. physically
> 6. perfection

b. Word 1 is **unlikeliest.** Spell **unlikeliest.** Get ready. (Signal.) *U-N-L-I-K-E-L-I-E-S-T.*

c. Word 2 is **mission.** Spell **mission.** Get ready. (Signal.) *M-I-S-S-I-O-N.*

d. (Repeat step c for: **3. complained, 4. accidentally, 5. physically, 6. perfection.**)

e. (Erase the board.)

- Now spell those words without looking.

f. Word 1 is **unlikeliest.** Spell **unlikeliest.** Get ready. (Signal.) *U-N-L-I-K-E-L-I-E-S-T.*

g. Word 2 is **mission.** Spell **mission.** Get ready. (Signal.) *M-I-S-S-I-O-N.*

h. (Repeat step g for: **3. complained, 4. accidentally, 5. physically, 6. perfection.**)

i. (Give individual turns on: **1. unlikeliest, 2. mission, 3. complained, 4. accidentally, 5. physically, 6. perfection.**)

EXERCISE 1

Plural Variation

a. Let's say some words that have the sound /vvv/ in the plural.

b. My turn: The plural of **leaf** is (pause) **leaves.**

- The plural of **half** is (pause) **halves.**
- The plural of **thief** is (pause) **thieves.**

c. Your turn: What's the plural of **thief?** (Signal.) *Thieves.*

- What's the plural of **half?** (Signal.) *Halves.*
- What's the plural of **wolf?** (Signal.) *Wolves.*
- What's the plural of **calf?** (Signal.) *Calves.*
- (Repeat step c until firm.)

d. (Write on the board:)

> **leaf   leaves**

e. Listen: Some words that end in the sound /fff/ have the letters **v-e-s** in the plural.

- You can always hear the sound /vvv/ in the plural.

f. (Point to **leaf.**)

- Everybody, spell the word **leaf.** Get ready. (Signal.) *L-E-A-F.*
- Say the plural of **leaf.** (Signal.) *Leaves.*

g. Spell **leaves.** Get ready. (Signal.) *L-E-A-V-E-S.*

h. Everybody, spell the word **half.** Get ready. (Signal.) *H-A-L-F.*

- Say the plural of **half.** (Signal.) *Halves.*

i. Spell **halves.** Get ready. (Signal.) *H-A-L-V-E-S.*

EXERCISE 2

Sentence

a. (Write on the board:)

> **Their approach to acquiring knowledge fascinates me.**

- I'll read the sentence on the board. **Their approach to acquiring knowledge fascinates me.**
- Let's spell some of those words.

b. Spell **Their.** Get ready. (Signal.) *T-H-E-I-R.*

- Spell **approach.** Get ready. (Signal.) *A-P-P-R-O-A-C-H.*
- Spell **acquiring.** Get ready. (Signal.) *A-C-Q-U-I-R-I-N-G.*
- Spell **knowledge.** Get ready. (Signal.) *K-N-O-W-L-E-D-G-E.*
- Spell **fascinates.** Get ready. (Signal.) *F-A-S-C-I-N-A-T-E-S.*

c. (Erase the board.)

d. Now let's spell some of the words in that sentence without looking.

- Spell **Their.** Get ready. (Signal.) *T-H-E-I-R.*
- Spell **approach.** Get ready. (Signal.) *A-P-P-R-O-A-C-H.*
- Spell **acquiring.** Get ready. (Signal.) *A-C-Q-U-I-R-I-N-G.*
- Spell **knowledge.** Get ready. (Signal.) *K-N-O-W-L-E-D-G-E.*
- Spell **fascinates.** Get ready. (Signal.) *F-A-S-C-I-N-A-T-E-S.*

EXERCISE 3

Spelling Review

a. Get ready to spell and write some words.

b. Word 1 is **permission.**

- What word? (Signal.) *Permission.*
- Spell **permission.** Get ready. (Signal.) *P-E-R-M-I-S-S-I-O-N.*
- Write it.

c. Word 2 is **likelihood.**

- What word? (Signal.) *Likelihood.*
- Spell **likelihood.** Get ready. (Signal.) *L-I-K-E-L-I-H-O-O-D.*
- Write it.

d. (Repeat step c for: **3. observer, 4. defective, 5. unapproved, 6. extraction.**)

e. I'll spell each word.

- Put an **X** next to any word you missed and write that word correctly.
- (Spell each word twice. Write the words on the board as you spell them.)

> 1. permission   4. defective
> 2. likelihood   5. unapproved
> 3. observer   6. extraction

EXERCISE 1

Plural Variation

a. (Write on the board:)

> 1. thief
> 2. wife
> 3. loaf
> 4. wolf

- Copy the board. ✔
b. These four words end in the sound /fff/. After each word, write its plural word. ✔
c. We are going to check the words you just wrote. Cross out any word you missed and write that word correctly.
d. The first word is **thief.** Say the plural of **thief.** (Signal.) *Thieves.*
- Spell **thieves.** Get ready. (Signal.) *T-H-I-E-V-E-S.*
e. The next word is **wife.** Say the plural of **wife.** (Signal.) *Wives.*
- Spell **wives.** Get ready. (Signal.) *W-I-V-E-S.*
f. The next word is **loaf.** Say the plural of **loaf.** (Signal.) *Loaves.*
- Spell **loaves.** Get ready. (Signal.) *L-O-A-V-E-S.*
g. The next word is **wolf.** Say the plural of **wolf.** (Signal.) *Wolves.*
- Spell **wolves.** Get ready. (Signal.) *W-O-L-V-E-S.*

EXERCISE 2

Sentence

a. (Write on the board:)

> **Their approach to acquiring knowledge fascinates me.**

- I'll read the sentence on the board. **Their approach to acquiring knowledge fascinates me.**
- Let's spell some of those words.
b. Spell **Their.** Get ready. (Signal.) *T-H-E-I-R.*
- Spell **approach.** Get ready. (Signal.) *A-P-P-R-O-A-C-H.*
- Spell **acquiring.** Get ready. (Signal.) *A-C-Q-U-I-R-I-N-G.*

- Spell **knowledge.** Get ready. (Signal.) *K-N-O-W-L-E-D-G-E.*
- Spell **fascinates.** Get ready. (Signal.) *F-A-S-C-I-N-A-T-E-S.*
c. (Erase the board.)
d. Now let's spell some of the words in that sentence without looking.
- Spell **Their.** Get ready. (Signal.) *T-H-E-I-R.*
- Spell **approach.** Get ready. (Signal.) *A-P-P-R-O-A-C-H.*
- Spell **acquiring.** Get ready. (Signal.) *A-C-Q-U-I-R-I-N-G.*
- Spell **knowledge.** Get ready. (Signal.) *K-N-O-W-L-E-D-G-E.*
- Spell **fascinates.** Get ready. (Signal.) *F-A-S-C-I-N-A-T-E-S.*

EXERCISE 3

Sentence Variation

a. Get ready to write on lined paper.
- You are going to write a sentence made up of words you know how to spell. Put the right punctuation mark at the end of the sentence.
b. The sentence is **Those people are on the physical science committee.**
- Say that sentence. Get ready. (Signal.) *Those people are on the physical science committee.*
- (Repeat until firm.)
c. Write it. ✔
d. Get ready to check your spelling. Put an **X** next to any word you missed.
e. Spell **Those.** Get ready. (Signal.) *T-H-O-S-E.*
- Check it. ✔
f. Spell **people.** Get ready. (Signal.) *P-E-O-P-L-E.*
- Check it. ✔
- (Repeat for: **physical, science, committee.**)
g. What punctuation mark did you put at the end of the sentence? (Signal.) *A period.*
- Check it. ✔
h. Fix any words you missed.

EXERCISE 1

Word Introduction

a. (Write on the board:)

> void
> friend
> mobile
> temple
> proper
> please

b. Get ready to read these words.
- First word: **void.** What word? (Signal.) *Void.*
c. Next word: **friend.** What word? (Signal.) *Friend.*
- (Repeat for: **mobile, temple, proper, please.**)
d. Now spell those words.
- Spell **void.** Get ready. (Signal.) *V-O-I-D.*
e. Spell **friend.** Get ready. (Signal.) *F-R-I-E-N-D.*
- (Repeat for: **mobile, temple, proper, please.**)
f. (Erase the board.)
- Spell the words without looking.
g. Spell **void.** Get ready. (Signal.) *V-O-I-D.*
h. Spell **friend.** Get ready. (Signal.) *F-R-I-E-N-D.*
- (Repeat for: **mobile, temple, proper, please.**)
i. Get ready to write those words.
j. First word: **void.** Write it. ✔
- (Repeat for: **friend, mobile, temple, proper, please.**)

EXERCISE 2

Sentence

a. You're going to write this sentence. **Their approach to acquiring knowledge fascinates me.**
b. Say the sentence. Get ready. (Signal.) *Their approach to acquiring knowledge fascinates me.*
c. Write the sentence. ✔
d. (Write on the board:)

> **Their approach to acquiring knowledge fascinates me.**

e. Check your work. Make an **X** next to any word you got wrong. ✔

EXERCISE 3

Spelling Review

a. You're going to write words.
- Number your paper from 1 to 6. ✔
b. Word 1 is **translation.** Write it. ✔
c. Word 2 is **straightening.** Write it. ✔
d. (Repeat step c for: **3. wreckage, 4. prescription, 5. slippiest, 6. interesting.**)
e. Check your work. Make an **X** next to any word you got wrong.
f. Word 1. Spell **translation.** Get ready. (Tap for each letter.) *T-R-A-N-S-L-A-T-I-O-N.*
- (Repeat for: **2. straightening, 3. wreckage, 4. prescription, 5. slippiest, 6. interesting.**)

EXERCISE 1

Affix Introduction

a. (Write on the board:)

> 1. de + sign + ate =
> 2. medic + ate =
> 3. pulse + ate =

- All these words have the morphograph **ate**.
b. Number your paper from 1 to 3. ✔
c. Add the morphographs together to make new words. Write just the new words. ✔
d. Check your work. Make an **X** next to any word you got wrong.
e. Word 1. Spell **designate**. Get ready. (Tap for each letter.) *D-E-S-I-G-N-A-T-E.*
- (Repeat for: **2. medicate, 3. pulsate.**)

EXERCISE 2

Word Building

a. (Write on the board:)

> 1. dis + color + ate + ion = _____
> 2. in + fine + ate = _____
> 3. please + ure + able = _____
> 4. con + tent + ment = _____
> 5. re + spect + ful + ly = _____
> 6. per + cept + ion = _____

b. You're going to write the words that go in the blanks.
- Number your paper from 1 to 6. ✔
c. Word 1. Write **discoloration** on your paper. ✔
d. Do the rest of the words on your own. ✔
e. Check your work. Make an **X** next to any word you got wrong.
f. Word 1. Spell **discoloration**. Get ready. (Tap for each letter.) *D-I-S-C-O-L-O-R-A-T-I-O-N.*
- (Repeat for: **2. infinite, 3. pleasurable, 4. contentment, 5. respectfully, 6. perception.**)

EXERCISE 3

Prompted Review

a. (Write on the board:)

> 1. wolves
> 2. acquiring
> 3. permission
> 4. knowledge
> 5. wives
> 6. conscientious

b. Word 1 is **wolves**. Spell **wolves**. Get ready. (Signal.) *W-O-L-V-E-S.*
c. Word 2 is **acquiring**. Spell **acquiring**. Get ready. (Signal.) *A-C-Q-U-I-R-I-N-G.*
d. (Repeat step c for: **3. permission, 4. knowledge, 5. wives, 6. conscientious.**)
e. (Erase the board.)
- Now spell those words without looking.
f. Word 1 is **wolves**. Spell **wolves**. Get ready. (Signal.) *W-O-L-V-E-S.*
g. Word 2 is **acquiring**. Spell **acquiring**. Get ready. (Signal.) *A-C-Q-U-I-R-I-N-G.*
h. (Repeat step g for: **3. permission, 4. knowledge, 5. wives, 6. conscientious.**)
i. (Give individual turns on: **1. wolves, 2. acquiring, 3. permission, 4. knowledge, 5. wives, 6. conscientious.**)

EXERCISE 1

Nonword Base

a. (Write on the board:)

> **fuse**

- One morphograph that combines with other morphographs is **fuse.**
- What morphograph? (Signal.) *Fuse.*
- Spell **fuse.** Get ready. (Signal.) *F-U-S-E.*

b. Get ready to spell words that have the morphograph **fuse.**

c. First word: **refuse.**

- What's the first morphograph in **refuse?** (Signal.) *Re.*
- Next morphograph? (Signal.) *Fuse.*
- Spell **refuse.** Get ready. (Signal.) *R-E-F-U-S-E.*

d. Next word: **confuse.**

- What's the first morphograph in **confuse?** (Signal.) *Con.*
- Next morphograph? (Signal.) *Fuse.*
- Spell **confuse.** Get ready. (Signal.) *C-O-N-F-U-S-E.*

e. (For **transfusion** and **defuse,** have students identify each morphograph and spell each entire word.)

EXERCISE 2

Word Building

a. (Write on the board:)

> 1. tempt + ate + ion = _____
> 2. medic + ate = _____
> 3. re + serve + ate + ion = _____
> 4. re + late + ion = _____
> 5. sign + ate + ure = _____
> 6. de + sign + ate + ion = _____

b. You're going to write the words that go in the blanks.

- Number your paper from 1 to 6. ✔

c. Word 1. Write **temptation** on your paper. ✔

d. Do the rest of the words on your own. ✔

e. Check your work. Make an **X** next to any word you got wrong.

f. Word 1. Spell **temptation.** Get ready. (Tap for each letter.) *T-E-M-P-T-A-T-I-O-N.*

- (Repeat for: **2. medicate, 3. reservation, 4. relation, 5. signature, 6. designation.**)

EXERCISE 3

Prompted Review

a. (Write on the board:)

> 1. pleasure
> 2. unfriendly
> 3. commission
> 4. shelves
> 5. commitment
> 6. composure

b. Word 1 is **pleasure.** Spell **pleasure.** Get ready. (Signal.) *P-L-E-A-S-U-R-E.*

c. Word 2 is **unfriendly.** Spell **unfriendly.** Get ready. (Signal.) *U-N-F-R-I-E-N-D-L-Y.*

d. (Repeat step c for: **3. commission, 4. shelves, 5. commitment, 6. composure.**)

e. (Erase the board.)

- Now spell those words without looking.

f. Word 1 is **pleasure.** Spell **pleasure.** Get ready. (Signal.) *P-L-E-A-S-U-R-E.*

g. Word 2 is **unfriendly.** Spell **unfriendly.** Get ready. (Signal.) *U-N-F-R-I-E-N-D-L-Y.*

h. (Repeat step g for: **3. commission, 4. shelves, 5. commitment, 6. composure.**)

i. (Give individual turns on: **1. pleasure, 2. unfriendly, 3. commission, 4. shelves, 5. commitment, 6. composure.**)

LESSON 100

EXERCISE 1

Test

a. Today you have a spelling test. Number your lined paper from 1 through 10. ✔

b. Word 1 is **dismissal.** What word? (Signal.) *Dismissal.*
- Write the word **dismissal.** ✔

c. Word 2 is **unusually.** What word? (Signal.) *Unusually.*
- Write the word **unusually.** ✔

d. Word 3 is **knives.** What word? (Signal.) *Knives.*
- Write the word **knives.** ✔

e. Word 4 is **destruction.** What word? (Signal.) *Destruction.*
- Write the word **destruction.** ✔

f. Word 5 is **medication.** What word? (Signal.) *Medication.*
- Write the word **medication.** ✔

g. Word 6 is **permissive.** What word? (Signal.) *Permissive.*
- Write the word **permissive.** ✔

h. Word 7 is **likeliest.** What word? (Signal.) *Likeliest.*
- Write the word **likeliest.** ✔

i. Word 8 is **magically.** What word? (Signal.) *Magically.*
- Write the word **magically.** ✔

j. Word 9 is **unknown.** What word? (Signal.) *Unknown.*
- Write the word **unknown.** ✔

k. Word 10 is **courage.** What word? (Signal.) *Courage.*
- Write the word **courage.** ✔

l. Pick up your red pen. ✔
- Make an **X** next to any word you spelled wrong.
- (Write on the board:)

1. dismissal	6. permissive
2. unusually	7. likeliest
3. knives	8. magically
4. destruction	9. unknown
5. medication	10. courage

- Write the correct spelling next to any word you spelled wrong.
(Observe students and give feedback.)

EXERCISE 1

Word Introduction

a. (Write on the board:)

> pure
> temper
> vast
> image

b. Get ready to read these words.
- First word: **pure.** What word? (Signal.) *Pure.*
c. Next word: **temper.** What word? (Signal.) *Temper.*
- (Repeat for: **vast, image.**)
d. Now spell those words.
- Spell **pure.** Get ready. (Signal.) *P-U-R-E.*
e. Spell **temper.** Get ready. (Signal.) *T-E-M-P-E-R.*
- (Repeat for: **vast, image.**)
f. (Erase the board.)
- Spell the words without looking.
g. Spell **pure.** Get ready. (Signal.) *P-U-R-E.*
h. Spell **temper.** Get ready. (Signal.) *T-E-M-P-E-R.*
- (Repeat for: **vast, image.**)
i. Get ready to write those words.
j. First word: **pure.** Write it. ✔
- (Repeat for: **temper, vast, image.**)

EXERCISE 2

Affix Introduction

a. (Write on the board:)

> 1. be + side =
> 2. be + long =
> 3. be + have =

- All these words have the morphograph **be.**
b. Number your paper from 1 to 3. ✔
c. Add the morphographs together to make new words. Write just the new words. ✔
d. Check your work. Make an **X** next to any word you got wrong.
e. Word 1. Spell **beside.** Get ready. (Tap for each letter.) *B-E-S-I-D-E.*
- (Repeat for: **2. belong, 3. behave.**)

EXERCISE 3

Word Building

a. (Write on the board:)

> 1. re + fuse + al = _____
> 2. habit + ual = _____
> 3. trans + miss + ion = _____
> 4. ex + cept + ion = _____
> 5. act + ive + ate = _____
> 6. con + serve + ate + ion = _____

b. You're going to write the words that go in the blanks.
- Some of these words follow the final **e** rule. Some follow the doubling rule. Be careful.
- Number your paper from 1 to 6. ✔
c. Word 1. Write **refusal** on your paper. ✔
d. Do the rest of the words on your own. ✔
e. Check your work. Make an **X** next to any word you got wrong.
f. Word 1. Spell **refusal.** Get ready. (Tap for each letter.) *R-E-F-U-S-A-L.*
- (Repeat for: **2. habitual, 3. transmission, 4. exception, 5. activate, 6. conservation.**)

LESSON 102

EXERCISE 1

Nonword Base

a. (Write on the board:)

> **ply**

- One morphograph that combines with other morphographs is **ply.**
- What morphograph? (Signal.) *Ply.*
- Spell **ply.** Get ready. (Signal.) *P-L-Y.*

b. Get ready to spell words that have the morphograph **ply.**

c. First word: **reply.**

- What's the first morphograph in **reply?** (Signal.) *Re.*
- Next morphograph? (Signal.) *Ply.*
- Spell **reply.** Get ready. (Signal.) *R-E-P-L-Y.*

d. Next word: **comply.**

- What's the first morphograph in **comply?** (Signal.) *Com.*
- Next morphograph? (Signal.) *Ply.*
- Spell **comply.** Get ready. (Signal.) *C-O-M-P-L-Y.*

e. (For **imply** and **apply,** have students identify each morphograph and spell each entire word.)

EXERCISE 2

Sentence

a. (Write on the board:)

> **Adequately protecting the environment is a challenge.**

- I'll read the sentence on the board. **Adequately protecting the environment is a challenge.**
- Let's spell some of those words.

b. Spell **Adequately.** Get ready. (Signal.) *A-D-E-Q-U-A-T-E-L-Y.*

- Spell **protecting.** Get ready. (Signal.) *P-R-O-T-E-C-T-I-N-G.*
- Spell **environment.** Get ready. (Signal.) *E-N-V-I-R-O-N-M-E-N-T.*
- Spell **challenge.** Get ready. (Signal.) *C-H-A-L-L-E-N-G-E.*

c. Copy this sentence on lined paper.

d. (Pause, then check and correct.)

- Read the sentence you just copied. Get ready. (Signal.) *Adequately protecting the environment is a challenge.*

EXERCISE 3

Prompted Review

a. (Write on the board:)

> 1. medication
> 2. friendliest
> 3. fascinates
> 4. perfection
> 5. acquired
> 6. conscientious

b. Word 1 is **medication.** Spell **medication.** Get ready. (Signal.) *M-E-D-I-C-A-T-I-O-N.*

c. Word 2 is **friendliest.** Spell **friendliest.** Get ready. (Signal.) *F-R-I-E-N-D-L-I-E-S-T.*

d. (Repeat step c for: **3. fascinates, 4. perfection, 5. acquired, 6. conscientious.**)

e. (Erase the board.)

- Now spell those words without looking.

f. Word 1 is **medication.** Spell **medication.** Get ready. (Signal.) *M-E-D-I-C-A-T-I-O-N.*

g. Word 2 is **friendliest.** Spell **friendliest.** Get ready. (Signal.) *F-R-I-E-N-D-L-I-E-S-T.*

h. (Repeat step g for: **3. fascinates, 4. perfection, 5. acquired, 6. conscientious.**)

i. (Give individual turns on: **1. medication, 2. friendliest, 3. fascinates, 4. perfection, 5. acquired, 6. conscientious.**)

EXERCISE 1

Doubling Rule

a. Remember, you double the final **consonant** in a short word when the word ends **CVC** and the next morphograph begins with a **vowel.**

b. You're going to use that rule for some new words.

- Listen: When a word ends in a short **CVC** morphograph, use the doubling rule.
- Listen again: When a word ends in a short **CVC** morphograph, use the doubling rule.

c. Everybody, tell me the new rule. (Pause.) Get ready. (Signal.) *When a word ends in a short CVC morphograph, use the doubling rule.*

- (Repeat until firm.)

d. (Write on the board:)

> permit + ing =
> temper + ing
> recur + ing =
> forget + ing =
> wonder + ing =
> propel + ing =

e. (Point to **permit.**)

- **Permit** ends with a short **CVC** morphograph: **mit.** You double when you spell **permitting.**
- Everybody, spell **permitting.** Get ready. (Signal.) *P-E-R-M-I-T-T-I-N-G.*

f. (Point to **temper.**)

- **Temper** does not end with a short **CVC** morphograph. **Temper** is one morphograph. You don't double when you spell **tempering.**
- Everybody, spell **tempering.** Get ready. (Signal.) *T-E-M-P-E-R-I-N-G.*

g. (Point to **recur.**)

- **Recur** ends with a short **CVC** morphograph: **cur.** You double when you spell **recurring.**
- Everybody, spell **recurring.** Get ready. (Signal.) *R-E-C-U-R-R-I-N-G.*

h. (Point to **forget.**)

- **Forget** ends with a short **CVC** morphograph: **get.** You double when you spell **forgetting.**

- Everybody, spell **forgetting.** Get ready. (Signal.) *F-O-R-G-E-T-T-I-N-G.*

i. (Point to **wonder.**)

- **Wonder** does not end with a short **CVC** morphograph. **Wonder** is one morphograph. You don't double when you spell **wondering.**
- Everybody, spell **wondering.** Get ready. (Signal.) *W-O-N-D-E-R-I-N-G.*

j. (Point to **propel.**)

- **Propel** ends with a short **CVC** morphograph: **pel.** You double when you spell **propelling.**
- Everybody, spell **propelling.** Get ready. (Signal.) *P-R-O-P-E-L-L-I-N-G.*

EXERCISE 2

Sentence

a. (Write on the board:)

> **Adequately protecting the environment is a challenge.**

- I'll read the sentence on the board. **Adequately protecting the environment is a challenge.**
- Let's spell some of those words.

b. Spell **Adequately.** Get ready. (Signal.) *A-D-E-Q-U-A-T-E-L-Y.*

- Spell **protecting.** Get ready. (Signal.) *P-R-O-T-E-C-T-I-N-G.*
- Spell **environment.** Get ready. (Signal.) *E-N-V-I-R-O-N-M-E-N-T.*
- Spell **challenge.** Get ready. (Signal.) *C-H-A-L-L-E-N-G-E.*

c. (Erase the board.)

d. Now let's spell some of the words in that sentence without looking.

- Spell **Adequately.** Get ready. (Signal.) *A-D-E-Q-U-A-T-E-L-Y.*
- Spell **protecting.** Get ready. (Signal.) *P-R-O-T-E-C-T-I-N-G.*
- Spell **environment.** Get ready. (Signal.) *E-N-V-I-R-O-N-M-E-N-T.*
- Spell **challenge.** Get ready. (Signal.) *C-H-A-L-L-E-N-G-E.*

Word Building

a. (Write on the board:)

> 1. re + ply + ed = _____
> 2. temper + ate + ure = _____
> 3. dis + miss + ed = _____
> 4. temple + ate = _____
> 5. in + fect + ion = _____
> 6. un + ap + prove + ed = _____

b. You're going to write the words that go in the blanks.

- Number your paper from 1 to 6. ✔

c. Word 1. Write **replied** on your paper. ✔

d. Do the rest of the words on your own. ✔

e. Check your work. Make an **X** next to any word you got wrong.

f. Word 1. Spell **replied.** Get ready. (Tap for each letter.) *R-E-P-L-I-E-D.*

- (Repeat for: **2. temperature, 3. dismissed, 4. template, 5. infection, 6. unapproved.**)

EXERCISE 1

Doubling Rule

a. When a word ends in a short **CVC** morphograph, use the doubling rule.

b. (Write on the board:)

> 1. compel + ed =
> 2. forbid + en =
> 3. spirit + ual =
> 4. transmit + al =
> 5. refer + ed =
> 6. comic + al =

c. Copy the board to your paper, then circle the words that end with a short **CVC** morphograph. ✔

d. You should have circled **compel, forbid, transmit,** and **refer.**

• Write each word after the equal sign. ✔

e. (Change the board to show:)

> 1. (compel) + ed = **compelled**
> 2. (forbid) + en = **forbidden**
> 3. spirit + ual = **spiritual**
> 4. (transmit) + al = **transmittal**
> 5. (refer) + ed = **referred**
> 6. comic + al = **comical**

f. Check your work. Put an **X** next to any word you missed. ✔

EXERCISE 2

Sentence

a. (Write on the board:)

> **Adequately protecting the environment is a challenge.**

• I'll read the sentence on the board. **Adequately protecting the environment is a challenge.**

• Let's spell some of those words.

b. Spell **Adequately.** Get ready. (Signal.) *A-D-E-Q-U-A-T-E-L-Y.*

• Spell **protecting.** Get ready. (Signal.) *P-R-O-T-E-C-T-I-N-G.*

• Spell **environment.** Get ready. (Signal.) *E-N-V-I-R-O-N-M-E-N-T.*

• Spell **challenge.** Get ready. (Signal.) *C-H-A-L-L-E-N-G-E.*

c. (Erase the board.)

d. Now let's spell some of the words in that sentence without looking.

• Spell **Adequately.** Get ready. (Signal.) *A-D-E-Q-U-A-T-E-L-Y.*

• Spell **protecting.** Get ready. (Signal.) *P-R-O-T-E-C-T-I-N-G.*

• Spell **environment.** Get ready. (Signal.) *E-N-V-I-R-O-N-M-E-N-T.*

• Spell **challenge.** Get ready. (Signal.) *C-H-A-L-L-E-N-G-E.*

EXERCISE 3

Spelling Review

a. Get ready to spell and write some words.

b. Word 1 is **calves.**

• What word? (Signal.) *Calves.*

• Spell **calves.** Get ready. (Signal.) *C-A-L-V-E-S.*

• Write it. ✔

c. Word 2 is **knowledge.**

• What word? (Signal.) *Knowledge.*

• Spell **knowledge.** Get ready. (Signal.) *K-N-O-W-L-E-D-G-E.*

• Write it. ✔

d. (Repeat step c for: **3. expression, 4. intensively, 5. perfection, 6. fitting.**)

e. I'll spell each word.

• Put an **X** next to any word you missed and write that word correctly.

• (Spell each word twice. Write the words on the board as you spell them.)

> 1. calves   4. intensively
> 2. knowledge   5. perfection
> 3. expression   6. fitting

EXERCISE 1

Doubling Rule

a. When a word ends in a short **CVC** morphograph, use the doubling rule.

b. (Write on the board:)

> 1. habit + ual =
> 2. incur + ing =
> 3. transfer + ed =
> 4. expel + ing =
> 5. reason + able =
> 6. commit + ed =

c. Copy the board to your paper, then circle the words that end with a short **CVC** morphograph. ✔

d. You should have circled **incur, transfer, expel,** and **commit.**

• Write each word after the equal sign. ✔

e. (Change the board to show:)

> 1. habit + ual = **habitual**
> 2. (incur) + ing = **incurring**
> 3. (transfer) + ed = **transferred**
> 4. (expel) + ing = **expelling**
> 5. reason + able = **reasonable**
> 6. (commit) + ed = **committed**

f. Check your work. Put an **X** next to any word you missed. ✔

EXERCISE 2

Sentence

a. You're going to write this sentence: **Adequately protecting the environment is a challenge.**

b. Say the sentence. Get ready. (Signal.) *Adequately protecting the environment is a challenge.*

c. Write the sentence. ✔

d. (Write on the board:)

> **Adequately protecting the environment is a challenge.**

e. Check your work. Make an **X** next to any word you got wrong. ✔

EXERCISE 3

Prompted Review

a. (Write on the board:)

> 1. transferring
> 2. permitted
> 3. recurring
> 4. scientists
> 5. thoroughness
> 6. challenge

b. Word 1 is **transferring.** Spell **transferring.** Get ready. (Signal.) *T-R-A-N-S-F-E-R-R-I-N-G.*

c. Word 2 is **permitted.** Spell **permitted.** Get ready. (Signal.) *P-E-R-M-I-T-T-E-D.*

d. (Repeat step c for: **3. recurring, 4. scientists, 5. thoroughness, 6. challenge.**)

e. (Erase the board.)

• Now spell those words without looking.

f. Word 1 is **transferring.** Spell **transferring.** Get ready. (Signal.) *T-R-A-N-S-F-E-R-R-I-N-G.*

g. Word 2 is **permitted.** Spell **permitted.** Get ready. (Signal.) *P-E-R-M-I-T-T-E-D.*

h. (Repeat step g for: **3. recurring, 4. scientists, 5. thoroughness, 6. challenge.**)

i. (Give individual turns on: **1. transferring, 2. permitted, 3. recurring, 4. scientists, 5. thoroughness, 6. challenge.**)

EXERCISE 1

Affix Introduction

a. (Write on the board:)

> 1. im + part =
> 2. im + port =
> 3. im + prove =

- All these words have the morphograph **im.**
b. Number your paper from 1 to 3. ✔
c. Add the morphographs together to make new words. Write just the new words. ✔
d. Check your work. Make an **X** next to any word you got wrong.
e. Word 1. Spell **impart.** Get ready. (Tap for each letter.) *I-M-P-A-R-T.*
- (Repeat for: **2. import, 3. improve.**)

EXERCISE 2

Nonword Base

a. (Write on the board:)

> **vert**

- One morphograph that cannot stand alone is **vert.**
- What morphograph? (Signal.) *Vert.*
- Spell **vert.** Get ready. (Signal.) *V-E-R-T.*
b. Get ready to spell words that have the morphograph **vert.**
c. First word: **convert.**
- What's the first morphograph in **convert?** (Signal.) *Con.*
- Next morphograph? (Signal.) *Vert.*
- Spell **convert.** Get ready. (Signal.) *C-O-N-V-E-R-T.*
d. Next word: **subvert.**
- What's the first morphograph in **subvert?** (Signal.) *Sub.*
- Next morphograph? (Signal.) *Vert.*
- Spell **subvert.** Get ready. (Signal.) *S-U-B-V-E-R-T.*
e. (For **invert** and **revert,** have students identify each morphograph and spell each entire word.)

EXERCISE 3

Word Building

a. (Write on the board:)

> 1. e + value + ate =
> 2. pre + vent + ion =
> 3. pro + spect + ive =
> 4. re + source + ful =
> 5. sub + merge + ed =
> 6. trans + fuse + ion =
> 7. for + get + ing =

b. You're going to write the words that go in the blanks.
- Some of these words follow the final **e** rule. Some follow the doubling rule. Be careful.
- Number your paper from 1 to 7. ✔
c. Word 1. Write **evaluate** on your paper. ✔
d. Do the rest of the words on your own. ✔
e. Check your work. Make an **X** next to any word you got wrong.
f. Word 1. Spell **evaluate.** Get ready. (Tap for each letter.) *E-V-A-L-U-A-T-E.*
- (Repeat for: **2. prevention, 3. prospective, 4. resourceful, 5. submerged, 6. transfusion, 7. forgetting.**)

EXERCISE 1

Nonword Base

a. (Write on the board:)

> **lief**

- One morphograph that cannot stand alone is **lief.**
- What morphograph? (Signal.) *Lief.*
- Spell **lief.** Get ready. (Signal.) *L-I-E-F.*
b. Get ready to spell words that have the morphograph **lief.**
c. First word: **relief.**
- What's the first morphograph in **relief?** (Signal.) *Re.*
- Next morphograph? (Signal.) *Lief.*
- Spell **relief.** Get ready. (Signal.) *R-E-L-I-E-F.*
d. Next word: **belief.**
- What's the first morphograph in **belief?** (Signal.) *Be.*
- Next morphograph? (Signal.) *Lief.*
- Spell **belief.** Get ready. (Signal.) *B-E-L-I-E-F.*

EXERCISE 2

Nonword Base

a. (Write on the board:)

> **lieve**

- One morphograph that cannot stand alone is **lieve.**
- What morphograph? (Signal.) *Lieve.*
- Spell **lieve.** Get ready. (Signal.) *L-I-E-V-E.*
b. Get ready to spell words that have the morphograph **lieve.**
c. First word: **relieve.**
- What's the first morphograph in **relieve?** (Signal.) *Re.*
- Next morphograph? (Signal.) *Lieve.*
- Spell **relieve.** Get ready. (Signal.) *R-E-L-I-E-V-E.*
d. Next word: **believe.**
- What's the first morphograph in **believe?** (Signal.) *Be.*
- Next morphograph? (Signal.) *Lieve.*
- Spell **believe.** Get ready. (Signal.) *B-E-L-I-E-V-E.*

EXERCISE 3

Affix Introduction

a. (Write on the board:)

> 1. e + merge =
> 2. e + ject =
> 3. e + vent =

- All these words have the morphograph **e.**
b. Number your paper from 1 to 3. ✔
c. Add the morphographs together to make new words. Write just the new words. ✔
d. Check your work. Make an **X** next to any word you got wrong.
e. Word 1. Spell **emerge.** Get ready. (Tap for each letter.) *E-M-E-R-G-E.*
- (Repeat for: **2. eject, 3. event.**)

EXERCISE 4

Prompted Review

a. (Write on the board:)

> 1. environment
> 2. referring
> 3. activation
> 4. fascinates
> 5. wondering
> 6. applied

b. Word 1 is **environment.** Spell **environment.** Get ready. (Signal.) *E-N-V-I-R-O-N-M-E-N-T.*
c. Word 2 is **referring.** Spell **referring.** Get ready. (Signal.) *R-E-F-E-R-R-I-N-G.*
d. (Repeat step c for: **3. activation, 4. fascinates, 5. wondering, 6. applied.**)
e. (Erase the board.)
- Now spell those words without looking.
f. Word 1 is **environment.** Spell **environment.** Get ready. (Signal.) *E-N-V-I-R-O-N-M-E-N-T.*
g. Word 2 is **referring.** Spell **referring.** Get ready. (Signal.) *R-E-F-E-R-R-I-N-G.*
h. (Repeat step g for: **3. activation, 4. fascinates, 5. wondering, 6. applied.**)
i. (Give individual turns on: **1. environment, 2. referring, 3. activation, 4. fascinates, 5. wondering, 6. applied.**)

LESSON 108

EXERCISE 1

Nonword Base

a. (Write on the board:)

> **ceive**

- One morphograph that cannot stand alone is **ceive.**
- What morphograph? (Signal.) *Ceive.*
- Spell **ceive.** Get ready. (Signal.) *C-E-I-V-E.*

b. Get ready to spell words that have the morphograph **ceive.**

c. First word: **receive.**

- What's the first morphograph in **receive?** (Signal.) *Re.*
- Next morphograph? (Signal.) *Ceive.*
- Spell **receive.** Get ready. (Signal.) *R-E-C-E-I-V-E.*

d. Next word: **deceive.**

- What's the first morphograph in **deceive?** (Signal.) *De.*
- Next morphograph? (Signal.) *Ceive.*
- Spell **deceive.** Get ready. (Signal.) *D-E-C-E-I-V-E.*

e. (For **perceive** and **conceive,** have students identify each morphograph and spell each entire word.)

EXERCISE 2

Affix Introduction

a. (Write on the board:)

> 1. **ad + mit =**
> 2. **ad + vise =**
> 3. **ad + just =**

- All these words have the morphograph **ad.**

b. Number your paper from 1 to 3. ✔

c. Add the morphographs together to make new words. Write just the new words. ✔

d. Check your work. Make an **X** next to any word you got wrong.

e. Word 1. Spell **admit.** Get ready. (Tap for each letter.) *A-D-M-I-T.*
- (Repeat for: **2. advise, 3. adjust.**)

EXERCISE 3

Word Building

a. (Write on the board:)

> 1. **im + per + fect = _____**
> 2. **com + ply + ing = _____**
> 3. **temper + ate + ure = _____**
> 4. **con + fuse + ion = _____**
> 5. **please + ure = _____**
> 6. **sign + ate + ure = _____**

b. You're going to write the words that go in the blanks.

- Number your paper from 1 to 6. ✔

c. Word 1. Write **imperfect** on your paper. ✔

d. Do the rest of the words on your own. ✔

e. Check your work. Make an **X** next to any word you got wrong.

f. Word 1. Spell **imperfect.** Get ready. (Tap for each letter.) *I-M-P-E-R-F-E-C-T.*
- (Repeat for: **2. complying, 3. temperature, 4. confusion, 5. pleasure, 6. signature.**)

EXERCISE 1

Nonword Base

a. (Write on the board:)

> **sume**

- One morphograph that cannot stand alone is **sume.**
- What morphograph? (Signal.) *Sume.*
- Spell **sume.** Get ready. (Signal.) *S-U-M-E.*

b. Get ready to spell words that have the morphograph **sume.**

c. First word: **resume.**

- What's the first morphograph in **resume?** (Signal.) *Re.*
- Next morphograph? (Signal.) *Sume.*
- Spell **resume.** Get ready. (Signal.) *R-E-S-U-M-E.*

d. Next word: **consume.**

- What's the first morphograph in **consume?** (Signal.) *Con.*
- Next morphograph? (Signal.) *Sume.*
- Spell **consume.** Get ready. (Signal.) *C-O-N-S-U-M-E.*

e. (For **presume,** have students identify each morphograph and spell the entire word.)

EXERCISE 2

Affix Introduction

a. (Write on the board:)

> 1. sup + port =
> 2. sup + pose =
> 3. sup + ply =

- All these words have the morphograph **sup.**

b. Number your paper from 1 to 3. ✔

c. Add the morphographs together to make new words. Write just the new words. ✔

d. Check your work. Make an **X** next to any word you got wrong.

e. Word 1. Spell **support.** Get ready. (Tap for each letter.) *S-U-P-P-O-R-T.*

- (Repeat for: **2. suppose, 3. supply.**)

EXERCISE 3

Spelling Review

a. You're going to write words.

- Number your paper from 1 to 6. ✔

b. Word 1 is **fascinate.** Write it. ✔

c. Word 2 is **adjustment.** Write it. ✔

d. (Repeat step c for: **3. ejection, 4. advising, 5. signature, 6. perfection.**)

e. Check your work. Make an **X** next to any word you got wrong.

f. Word 1. Spell **fascinate.** Get ready. (Tap for each letter.) *F-A-S-C-I-N-A-T-E.*

- (Repeat for: **2. adjustment, 3. ejection, 4. advising, 5. signature, 6. perfection.**)

LESSON 110

EXERCISE 1

Test

a. Today you have a spelling test. Number your lined paper from 1 through 10. ✔
b. Word 1 is **subverted.** What word? (Signal.) *Subverted.*
- Write the word **subverted.** ✔
c. Word 2 is **behaving.** What word? (Signal.) *Behaving.*
- Write the word **behaving.** ✔
d. Word 3 is **replied.** What word? (Signal.) *Replied.*
- Write the word **replied.** ✔
e. Word 4 is **transferred.** What word? (Signal.) *Transferred.*
- Write the word **transferred.** ✔
f. Word 5 is **vastness.** What word? (Signal.) *Vastness.*
- Write the word **vastness.** ✔
g. Word 6 is **improperly.** What word? (Signal.) *Improperly.*
- Write the word **improperly.** ✔
h. Word 7 is **magically.** What word? (Signal.) *Magically.*
- Write the word **magically.** ✔

i. Word 8 is **gradual.** What word? (Signal.) *Gradual.*
- Write the word **gradual.** ✔
j. Word 9 is **treasure.** What word? (Signal.) *Treasure.*
- Write the word **treasure.** ✔
k. Word 10 is **strapping.** What word? (Signal.) *Strapping.*
- Write the word **strapping.** ✔
l. Pick up your red pen. ✔
Make an **X** next to any word you spelled wrong.
- (Write on the board:)

1. subverted	6. improperly
2. behaving	7. magically
3. replied	8. gradual
4. transferred	9. treasure
5. vastness	10. strapping

- Write the correct spelling next to any word you spelled wrong.
(Observe students and give feedback.)

EXERCISE 1

Morphograph Analysis

a. (Write on the board:)

> 1. relentless
> 2. incomplete
> 3. surround

b. Each of these words has a morphograph that you have not learned yet.

c. Word 1: **relentless.**

- The morphographs you know are **re** and **less.**

- What's the new morphograph? (Signal.) *Lent.*

d. Spell **relentless.** Get ready. (Signal.) *R-E-L-E-N-T-L-E-S-S.*

- (Repeat until firm.)

e. Word 2: **incomplete.**

- The morphographs you know are **in** and **com.**

- What's the new morphograph? (Signal.) *Plete.*

f. Spell **incomplete.** Get ready. (Signal.) *I-N-C-O-M-P-L-E-T-E.*

- (Repeat until firm.)

g. Word 3: **surround.**

- The morphograph you know is **round.**

- What's the new morphograph? (Signal.) *Sur.*

h. Spell **surround.** Get ready. (Signal.) *S-U-R-R-O-U-N-D.*

- (Repeat until firm.)

i. (Erase the board.)

j. Number your paper from 1 to 3. ✔

- Get ready to write those words without looking.

k. Word 1. Write **relentless.** ✔

l. Word 2. Write **incomplete.** ✔

m. Word 3. Write **surround.** ✔

n. Check your work. Make an **X** next to any word you got wrong.

o. Word 1. Spell **relentless.** Get ready. (Tap for each letter.) *R-E-L-E-N-T-L-E-S-S.*

- (Repeat for: **2. incomplete, 3. surround.**)

EXERCISE 2

Word Building

a. (Write on the board:)

> 1. sup + pose + ed + ly = _____
> 2. con + sume + er = _____
> 3. re + ceive + ing = _____
> 4. ad + mit + ed = _____
> 5. be + lieve + er = _____
> 6. im + prove + ment = _____

b. You're going to write the words that go in the blanks.

- Number your paper from 1 to 6. ✔

c. Word 1. Write **supposedly** on your paper. ✔

d. Do the rest of the words on your own. ✔

e. Check your work. Make an **X** next to any word you got wrong.

f. Word 1. Spell **supposedly.** Get ready. (Tap for each letter.) *S-U-P-P-O-S-E-D-L-Y.*

- (Repeat for: **2. consumer, 3. receiving, 4. admitted, 5. believer, 6. improvement.**)

Prompted Review

a. (Write on the board:)

> 1. environment
> 2. rhythmically
> 3. expelled
> 4. applied
> 5. unusually
> 6. consuming

b. Word 1 is **environment.** Spell **environment.** Get ready. (Signal.) *E-N-V-I-R-O-N-M-E-N-T.*

c. Word 2 is **rhythmically.** Spell **rhythmically.** Get ready. (Signal.) *R-H-Y-T-H-M-I-C-A-L-L-Y.*

d. (Repeat step c for: **3. expelled, 4. applied, 5. unusually, 6. consuming.**)

e. (Erase the board.)

• Now spell those words without looking.

f. Word 1 is **environment.** Spell **environment.** Get ready. (Signal.) *E-N-V-I-R-O-N-M-E-N-T.*

g. Word 2 is **rhythmically.** Spell **rhythmically.** Get ready. (Signal.) *R-H-Y-T-H-M-I-C-A-L-L-Y.*

h. (Repeat step g for: **3. expelled, 4. applied, 5. unusually, 6. consuming.**)

i. (Give individual turns on: **1. environment, 2. rhythmically, 3. expelled, 4. applied, 5. unusually, 6. consuming.**)

LESSON 112

EXERCISE 1

Sentence Variation

a. Get ready to write on lined paper.
- You are going to write a sentence made up of words you know how to spell. Put the right punctuation mark at the end of the sentence.
b. The sentence is **The image in the photograph shows an important event.**
- Say that sentence. Get ready. (Signal.) *The image in the photograph shows an important event.*
- (Repeat until firm.)
c. Write it. ✔
d. Get ready to check your spelling. Put an **X** next to any word you missed.
e. Spell **image.** Get ready. (Signal.) *I-M-A-G-E.*
- Check it. ✔
f. Spell **photograph.** Get ready. (Signal.) *P-H-O-T-O-G-R-A-P-H.*
- Check it. ✔
- (Repeat for: **shows, important, event.**)
g. What punctuation mark did you put at the end of the sentence? (Signal.) *A period.*
- Check it. ✔
h. Fix any words you missed.

EXERCISE 2

Word Building

a. (Write on the board:)

> 1. im + ply + ed = _____
> 2. vert + ic + al = _____
> 3. de + plete + ed = _____
> 4. port + able = _____
> 5. be + long + ing = _____
> 6. trans + mit + ed = _____

b. You're going to write the words that go in the blanks.
- Number your paper from 1 to 6. ✔
c. Word 1. Write **implied** on your paper. ✔
d. Do the rest of the words on your own. ✔
e. Check your work. Make an **X** next to any word you got wrong.
f. Word 1. Spell **implied.** Get ready. (Tap for each letter.) *I-M-P-L-I-E-D.*
- (Repeat for: **2. vertical, 3. depleted, 4. portable, 5. belonging, 6. transmitted.**)

EXERCISE 3

Prompted Review

a. (Write on the board:)

> 1. conservation
> 2. surfacing
> 3. thoroughness
> 4. saltiest
> 5. temperature
> 6. believable

b. Word 1 is **conservation.** Spell **conservation.** Get ready. (Signal.) *C-O-N-S-E-R-V-A-T-I-O-N.*
c. Word 2 is **surfacing.** Spell **surfacing.** Get ready. (Signal.) *S-U-R-F-A-C-I-N-G.*
d. (Repeat step c for: **3. thoroughness, 4. saltiest, 5. temperature, 6. believable.**)
e. (Erase the board.)
- Now spell those words without looking.
f. Word 1 is **conservation.** Spell **conservation.** Get ready. (Signal.) *C-O-N-S-E-R-V-A-T-I-O-N.*
g. Word 2 is **surfacing.** Spell **surfacing.** Get ready. (Signal.) *S-U-R-F-A-C-I-N-G.*
h. (Repeat step g for: **3. thoroughness, 4. saltiest, 5. temperature, 6. believable.**)
i. (Give individual turns on: **1. conservation, 2. surfacing, 3. thoroughness, 4. saltiest, 5. temperature, 6. believable.**)

EXERCISE 1

Morphograph Analysis

a. (Write on the board:)

> 1. surprise
> 2. instantly
> 3. friendship

b. Each of these words has a morphograph that you have not learned yet.
c. Word 1: **surprise.**
• The morphograph you know is **sur.**
• What's the new morphograph? (Signal.) *Prise.*
d. Spell **surprise.** Get ready. (Signal.) *S-U-R-P-R-I-S-E.*
• (Repeat until firm.)
e. Word 2: **instantly.**
• The morphographs you know are **in** and **ly.**
• What's the new morphograph? (Signal.) *Stant.*
f. Spell **instantly.** Get ready. (Signal.) *I-N-S-T-A-N-T-L-Y.*
• (Repeat until firm.)
g. Word 3: **friendship.**
• The morphograph you know is **friend.**
• What's the new morphograph? (Signal.) *Ship.*
h. Spell **friendship.** Get ready. (Signal.) *F-R-I-E-N-D-S-H-I-P.*
• (Repeat until firm.)
i. (Erase the board.)
j. Number your paper from 1 to 3. ✔
• Get ready to write those words without looking.
k. Word 1: Write **surprise.** ✔
l. Word 2: Write **instantly.** ✔
m. Word 3: Write **friendship.** ✔
n. Check your work. Make an **X** next to any word you got wrong.
o. Word 1. Spell **surprise.** Get ready. (Tap for each letter.) *S-U-R-P-R-I-S-E.*
• (Repeat for: **2. instantly, 3. friendship.**)

EXERCISE 2

Word Building)

a. (Write on the board:)

> 1. ex + pel + ed = _____
> 2. im + per + fect + ion = _____
> 3. govern + ment + al = _____
> 4. sub + miss + ion = _____
> 5. per + ceive + ing = _____
> 6. com + pose + ed = _____

b. You're going to write the words that go in the blanks.
• Number your paper from 1 to 6. ✔
c. Word 1. Write **expelled** on your paper. ✔
d. Do the rest of the words on your own. ✔
e. Check your work. Make an **X** next to any word you got wrong.
f. Word 1. Spell **expelled.** Get ready. (Tap for each letter.) *E-X-P-E-L-L-E-D.*
• (Repeat for: **2. imperfection, 3. governmental, 4. submission, 5. perceiving, 6. composed.**)

EXERCISE 3

Spelling Review

a. Get ready to spell words.
b. Word 1 is **incomplete.**
• What word? (Signal.) *Incomplete.*
• Spell **incomplete.** Get ready. (Signal.) *I-N-C-O-M-P-L-E-T-E.*
c. Word 2 is **unstoppable.**
• What word? (Signal.) *Unstoppable.*
• Spell **unstoppable.** Get ready. (Signal.) *U-N-S-T-O-P-P-A-B-L-E.*
d. (Repeat step c for: **3. halves, 4. interviewer, 5. photographer, 6. transferred.**)
e. (Give individual turns on: **1. incomplete, 2. unstoppable, 3. halves, 4. interviewer, 5. photographer, 6. transferred.**)

LESSON 114

EXERCISE 1

Sentence Variation

a. Get ready to write on lined paper.
- You are going to write a sentence made up of words you know how to spell. Put the right punctuation mark at the end of the sentence.

b. The sentence is **The committee thought that the children were physically unhealthy.**
- Say that sentence. Get ready. (Signal.) *The committee thought that the children were physically unhealthy.*
- (Repeat until firm.)

c. Write it. ✔

d. Get ready to check your spelling. Put an **X** next to any word you missed.

e. Spell **committee.** Get ready. (Signal.) *C-O-M-M-I-T-T-E-E.*
- Check it. ✔

f. Spell **thought.** Get ready. (Signal.) *T-H-O-U-G-H-T.*
- Check it. ✔
- (Repeat for: **that, children, were, physically, unhealthy.**)

g. What punctuation mark did you put at the end of the sentence? (Signal.) *A period.*
- Check it. ✔

h. Fix any words you missed.

EXERCISE 2

Word Building

a. (Write on the board:)

> 1. con + tract + ion = _____
> 2. de + struct + ive = _____
> 3. in + vent + ive = _____
> 4. de + ceive + ed = _____
> 5. for + get + ing = _____
> 6. dis + honest + ly = _____

b. You're going to write the words that go in the blanks.
- Number your paper from 1 to 6. ✔

c. Word 1. Write **contraction** on your paper. ✔

d. Do the rest of the words on your own. ✔

e. Check your work. Make an **X** next to any word you got wrong.

f. Word 1. Spell **contraction.** Get ready. (Tap for each letter.) *C-O-N-T-R-A-C-T-I-O-N.*
- (Repeat for: **2. destructive, 3. inventive, 4. deceived, 5. forgetting, 6. dishonestly.**)

EXERCISE 3

Prompted Review

a. (Write on the board:)

> 1. emotional
> 2. environmental
> 3. completed
> 4. believing
> 5. surprising
> 6. committed

b. Word 1 is **emotional.** Spell **emotional.** Get ready. (Signal.) *E-M-O-T-I-O-N-A-L.*

c. Word 2 is **environmental.** Spell **environmental.** Get ready. (Signal.) *E-N-V-I-R-O-N-M-E-N-T-A-L.*

d. (Repeat step c for: **3. completed, 4. believing, 5. surprising, 6. committed.**)

e. (Erase the board.)
- Now spell those words without looking.

f. Word 1 is **emotional.** Spell **emotional.** Get ready. (Signal.) *E-M-O-T-I-O-N-A-L.*

g. Word 2 is **environmental.** Spell **environmental.** Get ready. (Signal.) *E-N-V-I-R-O-N-M-E-N-T-A-L.*

h. (Repeat step g for: **3. completed, 4. believing, 5. surprising, 6. committed.**)

i. (Give individual turns on: **1. emotional, 2. environmental, 3. completed, 4. believing, 5. surprising, 6. committed.**)

EXERCISE 1

Morphograph Analysis

a. (Write on the board:)

> 1. automobile
> 2. telegraph
> 3. section

b. Each of these words has a morphograph that you have not learned yet.
c. Word 1: **automobile.**
 • The morphograph you know is **mobile.**
 • What's the new morphograph? (Signal.) *Auto.*
d. Spell **automobile.** Get ready. (Signal.) *A-U-T-O-M-O-B-I-L-E.*
 • (Repeat until firm.)
e. Word 2: **telegraph.**
 • The morphograph you know is **graph.**
 • What's the new morphograph? (Signal.) *Tele.*
f. Spell **telegraph.** Get ready. (Signal.) *T-E-L-E-G-R-A-P-H.*
 • (Repeat until firm.)
g. Word 3: **section.**
 • The morphograph you know is **ion.**
 • What's the new morphograph? (Signal.) *Sect.*
h. Spell **section.** Get ready. (Signal.) *S-E-C-T-I-O-N.*
 • (Repeat until firm.)
i. (Erase the board.)
j. Number your paper from 1 to 3. ✔
 • Get ready to write those words without looking.
k. Word 1. Write **automobile.** ✔
l. Word 2. Write **telegraph.** ✔
m. Word 3. Write **section.** ✔
n. Check your work. Make an **X** next to any word you got wrong.
o. Word 1. Spell **automobile.** Get ready. (Tap for each letter.) *A-U-T-O-M-O-B-I-L-E.*
 • (Repeat for: **2. telegraph, 3. section.**)

EXERCISE 2

Word Building

a. (Write on the board:)

> 1. com + mit + ed = _____
> 2. inter + view + er = _____
> 3. at + tract + ive = _____
> 4. ob + struct + ion = _____
> 5. for + give + en = _____
> 6. com + pel + ing = _____

b. You're going to write the words that go in the blanks.
 • Number your paper from 1 to 6. ✔
c. Word 1. Write **committed** on your paper. ✔
d. Do the rest of the words on your own. ✔
e. Check your work. Make an **X** next to any word you got wrong.
f. Word 1. Spell **committed.** Get ready. (Tap for each letter.) *C-O-M-M-I-T-T-E-D.*
 • (Repeat for: **2. interviewer, 3. attractive, 4. obstruction, 5. forgiven, 6. compelling.**)

EXERCISE 3

Spelling Review

a. Get ready to spell words.
b. Word 1 is **imperfect.**
 • What word? (Signal.) *Imperfect.*
 • Spell **imperfect.** Get ready. (Signal.) *I-M-P-E-R-F-E-C-T.*
c. Word 2 is **wolves.**
 • What word? (Signal.) *Wolves.*
 • Spell **wolves.** Get ready. (Signal.) *W-O-L-V-E-S.*
d. (Repeat step c for: **3. forgotten, 4. applied, 5. temperature, 6. relation.**)
e. (Give individual turns on: **1. imperfect, 2. wolves, 3. forgotten, 4. applied, 5. temperature, 6. relation.**)

LESSON 116

EXERCISE 1

Sentence Variation

a. Get ready to write on lined paper.
- You are going to write a sentence made up of words you know how to spell. Put the right punctuation mark at the end of the sentence.

b. The sentence is **The government had no objection to the provision yesterday.**
- Say that sentence. Get ready. (Signal.) *The government had no objection to the provision yesterday.*
- (Repeat until firm.)

c. Write it on the line. ✔

d. Get ready to check your spelling. Put an **X** next to any word you missed.

e. Spell **government.** Get ready. (Signal.) *G-O-V-E-R-N-M-E-N-T.*
- Check it. ✔

f. Spell **had.** Get ready. (Signal.) *H-A-D.*
- Check it. ✔
- (Repeat for: **objection, provision, yesterday.**)

g. What punctuation mark did you put at the end of the sentence? (Signal.) *A period.*
- Check it. ✔

h. Fix any words you missed.

EXERCISE 2

Word Building

a. (Write on the board:)

> 1. dis + sect + ion = _____
> 2. tele + phone = _____
> 3. con + stant = _____
> 4. de + plete + ed = _____
> 5. re + lieve + ed = _____
> 6. pro + tect + ion = _____

b. You're going to write the words that go in the blanks.
- Number your paper from 1 to 6. ✔

c. Word 1. Write **dissection** on your paper. ✔

d. Do the rest of the words on your own. ✔

e. Check your work. Make an **X** next to any word you got wrong.

f. Word 1. Spell **dissection.** Get ready. (Tap for each letter.) *D-I-S-S-E-C-T-I-O-N.*
- (Repeat for: **2. telephone, 3. constant, 4. depleted, 5. relieved, 6. protection.**)

EXERCISE 3

Prompted Review

a. (Write on the board:)

> 1. receiving
> 2. intersect
> 3. signature
> 4. surprising
> 5. apartment
> 6. inactively

b. Word 1 is **receiving.** Spell **receiving.** Get ready. (Signal.) *R-E-C-E-I-V-I-N-G.*

c. Word 2 is **intersect.** Spell **intersect.** Get ready. (Signal.) *I-N-T-E-R-S-E-C-T.*

d. (Repeat step c for: **3. signature, 4. surprising, 5. apartment, 6. inactively.**)

e. (Erase the board.)
- Now spell those words without looking.

f. Word 1 is **receiving.** Spell **receiving.** Get ready. (Signal.) *R-E-C-E-I-V-I-N-G.*

g. Word 2 is **intersect.** Spell **intersect.** Get ready. (Signal.) *I-N-T-E-R-S-E-C-T.*

h. (Repeat step g for: **3. signature, 4. surprising, 5. apartment, 6. inactively.**)

i. (Give individual turns on: **1. receiving, 2. intersect, 3. signature, 4. surprising, 5. apartment, 6. inactively.**)

LESSON 117

EXERCISE 1

Morphograph Analysis

a. (Write on the board:)

> 1. motion
> 2. predict
> 3. incision

b. Each of these words has a morphograph that you have not learned yet.
- Note: Two of the new morphographs end with the letter **e**. Be careful.
c. Word 1: **motion.**
- The morphograph you know is **i-o-n.**
- What's the new morphograph? (Signal.) *Mote.*
- The new morphograph is **mote: m-o-t-e.**
d. Spell **motion.** Get ready. (Signal.) *M-O-T-I-O-N.*
- (Repeat until firm.)
e. Word 2: **predict.**
- The morphograph you know is **pre.**
- What's the new morphograph? (Signal.) *Dict.*
f. Spell **predict.** Get ready. (Signal.) *P-R-E-D-I-C-T.*
- (Repeat until firm.)
g. Word 3: **incision.**
- The morphographs you know are **in** and **i-o-n.**
- What's the new morphograph? (Signal.) *Cise.*
- The new morphograph is **cise: c-i-s-e.**
h. Spell **incision.** Get ready. (Signal.) *I-N-C-I-S-I-O-N.*
- (Repeat until firm.)
i. (Erase the board.)
j. Number your paper from 1 to 3. ✔
- Get ready to write those words without looking.
k. Word 1. Write **motion.** ✔
l. Word 2. Write **predict.** ✔
m. Word 3. Write **incision.** ✔
n. Check your work. Make an **X** next to any word you got wrong.
o. Word 1. Spell **motion.** Get ready. (Tap for each letter.) *M-O-T-I-O-N.*
- (Repeat for: **2. predict, 3. incision.**)

EXERCISE 2

Word Building

a. (Write on the board:)

> 1. inter + sect + ion = _____
> 2. com + pel + ing = _____
> 3. re + quire + ment = _____
> 4. con + side + er + ate + ion = ____
> 5. un + sur + pass + ed = _____
> 6. sup + ply + er = _____

b. You're going to write the words that go in the blanks.
- Number your paper from 1 to 6. ✔
c. Word 1. Write **intersection** on your paper. ✔
d. Do the rest of the words on your own. ✔
e. Check your work. Make an **X** next to any word you got wrong.
f. Word 1. Spell **intersection.** Get ready. (Tap for each letter.) *I-N-T-E-R-S-E-C-T-I-O-N.*
- (Repeat for: **2. compelling, 3. requirement, 4. consideration, 5. unsurpassed, 6. supplier.**)

EXERCISE 3

Spelling Review

a. Get ready to spell words.
b. Word 1 is **signal.**
- What word? (Signal.) *Signal.*
- Spell **signal.** Get ready. (Signal.) *S-I-G-N-A-L.*
c. Word 2 is **attracted.**
- What word? (Signal.) *Attracted.*
- Spell **attracted.** Get ready. (Signal.) *A-T-T-R-A-C-T-E-D.*
d. (Repeat step c for: **3. compelling, 4. surrounded, 5. misspelled, 6. compression.**)
e. (Give individual turns on: **1. signal, 2. attracted, 3. compelling, 4. surrounded, 5. misspelled, 6. compression.**)

EXERCISE 1

Morphograph Analysis

a. (Write on the board:)

> 1. partial
> 2. confession
> 3. instance

b. Each of these words has a morphograph that you have not learned yet.

c. Word 1: **partial.**
- The morphograph you know is **part.**
- What's the new morphograph? (Signal.) *al.*

d. Spell **partial.** Get ready. (Signal.) *P-A-R-T-I-A-L.*
- (Repeat until firm.)

e. Word 2: **confession.**
- The morphographs you know are **con** and **i-o-n.**
- What's the new morphograph? (Signal.) *Fess.*

f. Spell **confession.** Get ready. (Signal.) *C-O-N-F-E-S-S-I-O-N.*
- (Repeat until firm.)

g. Word 3: **instance.**
- The morphograph you know is **in.**
- What's the new morphograph? (Signal.) *Stance.*

h. Spell **instance.** Get ready. (Signal.) *I-N-S-T-A-N-C-E.*
- (Repeat until firm.)

i. (Erase the board.)

j. Number your paper from 1 to 3. ✔
- Get ready to write those words without looking.

k. Word 1. Write **partial.** ✔

l. Word 2. Write **confession.** ✔

m. Word 3. Write **instance.** ✔

n. Check your work. Make an **X** next to any word you got wrong.

o. Word 1. Spell **partial.** Get ready. (Tap for each letter.) *P-A-R-T-I-A-L.*
- (Repeat for: **2. confession, 3. instance.**)

EXERCISE 2

Word Building

a. (Write on the board:)

> 1. pro + mote + ion = _____
> 2. de + cise + ion = _____
> 3. in + tense + ive = _____
> 4. court + ship = _____
> 5. com + mit + ment = _____
> 6. ob + ject + ion + able = _____

b. You're going to write the words that go in the blanks.
- Number your paper from 1 to 6. ✔

c. Word 1. Write **promotion** on your paper. ✔

d. Do the rest of the words on your own. ✔

e. Check your work. Make an **X** next to any word you got wrong.

f. Word 1. Spell **promotion.** Get ready. (Tap for each letter.) *P-R-O-M-O-T-I-O-N.*
- (Repeat for: **2. decision, 3. intensive, 4. courtship, 5. commitment, 6. objectionable.**)

EXERCISE 3

Spelling Review

a. You're going to write words.
- Number your paper from 1 to 6. ✔

b. Word 1 is **conscientious.** Write it. ✔

c. Word 2 is **spherical.** Write it. ✔

d. (Repeat step c for: **3. transfusion, 4. loaves, 5. complained, 6. thorough.**)

e. Check your work. Make an **X** next to any word you got wrong.

f. Word 1. Spell **conscientious.** Get ready. (Tap for each letter.) *C-O-N-S-C-I-E-N-T-I-O-U-S.*
- (Repeat for: **2. spherical, 3. transfusion, 4. loaves, 5. complained, 6. thorough.**)

EXERCISE 1

Sentence

a. Get ready to write on lined paper.

• You are going to write a sentence made up of words you know how to spell. Put the right punctuation mark at the end of the sentence.

b. The sentence is **The scientists disregarded the advice of the government with respect to the project.**

• Say that sentence. Get ready. (Signal.) *The scientists disregarded the advice of the government with respect to the project.*

• (Repeat until firm.)

c. Write it. ✔

d. Get ready to check your spelling. Put an **X** next to any word you missed.

e. Spell **scientists.** Get ready. (Signal.) *S-C-I-E-N-T-I-S-T-S.*

• Check it. ✔

f. Spell **disregarded.** Get ready. (Signal.) *D-I-S-R-E-G-A-R-D-E-D.*

• Check it. ✔

• (Repeat for: **advice, government, with, respect, project.**)

g. What punctuation mark did you put at the end of the sentence? (Signal.) *A period.*

• Check it. ✔

h. Fix any words you missed.

EXERCISE 2

Word Building

a. (Write on the board:)

> 1. part + ial + ly = _____
> 2. dict + ate + ion = _____
> 3. brother + hood = _____
> 4. trans + gress + ion = _____
> 5. pro + fess + ion + al = _____
> 6. con + cise + ly = _____

b. You're going to write the words that go in the blanks.

• Number your paper from 1 to 6. ✔

c. Word 1. Write **partially** on your paper. ✔

d. Do the rest of the words on your own. ✔

e. Check your work. Make an **X** next to any word you got wrong.

f. Word 1. Spell **partially.** Get ready. (Tap for each letter.) *P-A-R-T-I-A-L-L-Y.*

• (Repeat for: **2. dictation, 3. brotherhood, 4. transgression, 5. professional, 6. concisely.**)

EXERCISE 3

Spelling Review

a. You're going to write words.

• Number your paper from 1 to 6. ✔

b. Word 1 is **strengthen.** Write it. ✔

c. Word 2 is **critically.** Write it. ✔

d. (Repeat step c for: **3. dangerous, 4. physical, 5. ejection, 6. island.**)

e. Check your work. Make an **X** next to any word you got wrong.

f. Word 1. Spell **strengthen.** Get ready. (Tap for each letter.) *S-T-R-E-N-G-T-H-E-N.*

• (Repeat for: **2. critically, 3. dangerous, 4. physical, 5. ejection, 6. island.**)

EXERCISE 1

Test

a. Today you have a spelling test. Number your lined paper from 1 through 10. ✔

b. Word 1 is **receive.** What word? (Signal.) *Receive.*
* Write the word **receive.** ✔

c. Word 2 is **scientist.** What word? (Signal.) *Scientist.*
* Write the word **scientist.** ✔

d. Word 3 is **magical.** What word? (Signal.) *Magical.*
* Write the word **magical.** ✔

e. Word 4 is **transported.** What word? (Signal.) *Transported.*
* Write the word **transported.** ✔

f. Word 5 is **replied.** What word? (Signal.) *Replied.*
* Write the word **replied.** ✔

g. Word 6 is **transmitting.** What word? (Signal.) *Transmitting.*
* Write the word **transmitting.** ✔

h. Word 7 is **requirement.** What word? (Signal.) *Requirement.*
* Write the word **requirement.** ✔

i. Word 8 is **shown.** What word? (Signal.) *Shown.*
* Write the word **shown.** ✔

j. Word 9 is **assistants.** What word? (Signal.) *Assistants.*
* Write the word **assistants.** ✔

k. Word 10 is **furiously.** What word? (Signal.) *Furiously.*
* Write the word **furiously.** ✔

l. Pick up your red pen. ✔
Make an **X** next to any word you spelled wrong.
* (Write on the board:)

1. receive	6. transmitting
2. scientist	7. requirement
3. magical	8. shown
4. transported	9. assistants
5. replied	10. furiously

* Write the correct spelling next to any word you spelled wrong.
(Observe students and give feedback.)